ALL-TIME FAVORITES
COOKBOOK

VIVIAN A. WUDSKE, Editor
Ralph Genovese, Production coordinator

Published by Paramount Publishing, Inc.
All inquiries and correspondence should be directed to
Suite 413, Building B
800 Roosevelt Road
Glen Ellyn, Illinois 60137

Manufactured in the United States of America

Tenth Printing, May 1982

Library of Congress catalog card number: 78-63157
ISBN: 0-918668-02-6

TABLE OF CONTENTS PAGE NO.

SOUPS AND CHOWDERS

What could be nicer than to come home and smell the delightful aroma of a nourishing soup or chowder that has been cooking for a time??? Easy to prepare and delicious for a cool day any season of the year. With hearty soups like chowder and bisque, you need only to choose foods from the bread and fruit group to complete the meal. HAVE FUN!!!

PACIFIC SEAFOOD CHOWDER
(Pictured, Page 4)

1 ½ pounds genuine North Pacific
   halibut, fresh or frozen
1 (7-½ ounces) can Alaska King crab or
   1 (6 ounces) package frozen Alaska
      King crab
3 medium potatoes
1 large sweet Spanish onion
3/4 cup chopped celery
1/4 cup chopped green pepper
2 cloves garlic, minced
1/4 cup butter
2 (16 ounces) cans tomatoes
2 cups clam-tomato juice
1 ½ teaspoons salt
1/4 teaspoon pepper
1/4 teaspoon thyme
1/4 teaspoon marjoram
1 dozen small hard-shell clams (optional)
Chopped parsley

Defrost halibut, if frozen. Cut into 1-inch chunks. Drain canned crab and slice. Or defrost, drain and slice frozen crab. Peel potatoes and cut into ½-inch pieces. Peel and thinly slice onion. Saute onion, celery, green pepper and garlic in butter. Add tomatoes, clam-tomato juice and seasonings. Cover and simmer 30 minutes. Add halibut, potatoes and clams. Cover and simmer an additional 8 to 10 minutes, or until halibut and potatoes are done and clam shells open. Add crab and heat through. Sprinkle with chopped parsley.
Makes 8 servings.

RICH TURKEY BROTH

From left-over roast turkey, strip as much turkey meat as possible from bones, and package and refrigerate it (to be used within a day or two) or freeze for later use. Put bones and skin into a large kettle and barely cover with cold water. Add 1 chicken bouillon cube, 1 teaspoon salt, 12 peppercorns, 4 cloves, 1 stalk celery, 1 carrot, and 1 small onion, all cut up. Cover and simmer for 2 or 3 hours or until meat falls from bones. Strain broth and use immediately or refrigerate for use within a day or two, or freeze for later use.

TURKEY VEGETABLE NOODLE SOUP

2 quarts turkey broth
1 cup potatoes, cubed
1 cup carrots, sliced
1 cup, celery, sliced
1/4 cup chopped onion
1 package (10 ounces) frozen baby lima beans
1 teaspoon salt
1 cup uncooked noodles
2 cups turkey meat, cut up

Add vegetables to turkey broth along with salt and noodles and simmer 15 minutes. Add turkey, heat through and serve. Makes 6 servings.

GOLDEN CHEESE SOUP

1/4 cup water
2 tablespoons butter
1 package (10 ounces) frozen whole kernel corn
½ cup shredded carrot
1/4 cup chopped onion
1/8 teaspoon pepper
2 cans (10-½ ounces each) condensed cream of potato soup
2 cups milk
1 cup (4 ounces) shredded Cheddar cheese
½ cup (2 ounces) shredded Provolone cheese
1 cup broccoli flowerets (optional)

Bring water, butter, corn, carrot, onion, and pepper to a boil in a 3-quart saucepan; cover and simmer 10 minutes. Stir in soup, then milk, Cheddar and Provolone cheeses and broccoli. Heat stirring occasionally, until cheese melts and serving temperature is reached. (Do not boil) Garnish with broccoli flowerets, if desired. Yields 7-8 Cups.

POTATO SOUP WITH BUTTER BALLS

6 servings, (1 cup each)
1 large onion, chopped
5 large potatoes, cut in small pieces
2 teaspoons salt
1 cup water
3 cups milk
pepper - to taste

Cook onion and potatoes in water, boiling gently, covered for 15 minutes, or until potatoes are tender. Mash potatoes and onions. Add milk and seasonings. Heat slowly to serving temperature, stirring occasionally to prevent sticking. Add butter balls to thicken slightly.

BUTTER BALLS

In small fry pan, heat 2 tablespoons butter or margarine, add 2 Tablespoons flour or enough to form small balls when cool. Form the balls and add to the potato soup.

CHILE CON CARNE

6 servings, about 3/4 cup each
1 tablespoon fat or oil
1 medium onion, chopped
1 clove garlic, minced
3 cups kidney beans, dry, cooked drained (about 1-1/4 cups dry)
1 teaspoon salt
½ pound ground beef
½ green pepper, chopped
2 cups (16-ounce can) tomatoes, cooked or canned
2 or 3 teaspoons chili powder

Heat fat in a large frypan. Add meat, onion, and green pepper; brown lightly. Add remaining ingredients. Cover and simmer about 25 minutes to blend flavors. To thicken, remove cover during last few minutes of cooking. (Note: Canned, drained kidney beans may be used in this recipe. if preferred.)

HAM-SUCCOTASH CHOWDER

6 servings, 1 cup each
2 cups ham or smoked shoulder, cooked, chopped
16-ounce can corn, drained
1/4 cup flour
1 large onion, sliced
1-½ cups water
16-ounce can lima beans, drained
1-½ cups vegetable liquid plus water
2 tablespoons margarine

Simmer meat in water in a large, covered saucepan 15 minutes. Add vegetables. Blend vegetable liquid gradually with the flour to make a smooth mixture; stir into chowder. Cook, stirring as needed, until thickened. Melt fat in frypan; add onion and cook until lightly browned. Top chowder with onion slices.

SAUSAGE CHOWDER

1 quart tomatoes, broken up
2 cans (16 oz.) kidney beans
1 lb. sausage
1 qt. water
1-½ teaspoons seasoning salt
½ teaspoon thyme
½ teaspoon garlic salt
1/8 teaspoon black pepper
1 large bay leaf
1 cup diced potatoes
½ green pepper, chopped

Brown sausage, breaking up into small pieces. Combine all except potato and green pepper in large kettle. Bring to boil. Simmer one hour. Then add chopped green pepper and diced potatoes. Simmer 20 minutes or until vegetables are tender. Serve piping hot with fresh saltine crackers. 6 to 8 servings.

BEEF-VEGETABLE SOUP

6 servings, 1-2/3 cups each
1 pound beef short ribs
2 teaspoons salt
2 cups tomatoes, fresh or canned (16-ounce can)
½ cup onion, sliced
3 cups mixed vegetables (such as peas, cabbage, celery, green beans, green pepper, okra, turnips, or corn)
7 cups water
1/8 teaspoon pepper
1 cup diced potatoes
3/4 cup carrots, diced

Combine meat, water, salt, and pepper in a large saucepan. Bring to a boil; cover and simmer until meat can be easily removed from bones. Remove bones; skim off excess fat. Add remaining ingredients. If canned or leftover vegetables are used, add them during the last few minutes of cooking. Cover and cook 35 minutes or until vegetables are tender.

LAMB CREOLE

6 servings
1-½ pounds lamb steaks
2 tablespoons butter or margarine
½ cup celery, chopped
½ teaspoon salt
½ teaspoon chili powder
1/3 cup flour
½ cup onion, sliced
1-½ cups tomatoes, cooked or canned
3/4 teaspoons celery salt

Preheat oven to 350 degrees F. (moderate). Roll steaks in flour. Brown steaks lightly in hot fat. Place steaks in a shallow baking dish. Combine remaining ingredients. Pour over steaks. Bake covered, 1 hour. Remove cover; bake 30 minutes longer, or until tender.

LENTIL OR SPLIT PEA SOUP

1 pound lentils or green split peas
1/4 pound bacon, diced
2 medium onions, thinly sliced
2 carrots, thinly sliced
1 cup celery, sliced
2 bay leaves
3 teaspoons salt
1/4 teaspoon thyme
1/4 teaspoon black pepper
2 quarts water
1 large potato, grated raw
Meaty ham bone, if available

Soak lentils or green split peas minimum of 3 hours or overnight. In large soup kettle, saute bacon pieces, onions, carrots, until onions are golden. Add lentils or split peas after rinsing and draining. Add celery, bay leaves and seasonings and 2 quarts water. Grate large potato, peeled, into mixture, add meaty ham bone. cover, simmer 3-4 hours. Discard bay leaves. Cut meat from ham bone and return meat to soup mixture. Serves 6 generously.

QUICK FRENCH ONION SOUP

6 servings, (½ cup each)
1 cup bread cubes
2 tablespoons fat or oil
4 beef bouillon cubes
2 tablespoons parmesan or blue cheese, grated
2 cups onions, thinly sliced
3 cups boiling water
1 tablespoon butter or margarine, melted

Toast bread cubes in a 325°F. oven (slow) until they are completely dried out and lightly browned. Brown onions lightly in fat. Combine boiling water and bouillon cubes in a 2-quart saucepan. Add onions. Simmer, covered, until onions are tender, about 15 minutes. Toss toasted bread cubes with fat and cheese and sprinkle on top of soup just before serving.

CAMP-OUT SOUP

(Pictured, Page 9)

2 pounds beef for stew, cut in 1-inch pieces
2 cans (11½ ounces each) condensed
    bean soup
4½ cups water
1 medium onion, chopped
2 teaspoons salt
1 teaspoon basil
1/4 teaspoon pepper
1 package (5½ ounces) dehydrated
    hash brown potatoes
2 cans (16 ounces each) tomatoes
2 medium carrots, thinly sliced

Combine bean soup and water in large Dutch oven or pot. Add beef cubes, onion, salt, basil and pepper and bring to boil. Reduce heat, cover tightly and simmer 1½ hours. Add potatoes, tomatoes and carrots and continue cooking, covered, 30 to 40 minutes or until beef and vegetables are tender, stirring occasionally. 8 to 10 servings.

FRANKLY SOUP

1 can (11½ ounces) condensed green pea soup
2½ cups milk
1 cup (4 ounces) shredded Provolone cheese
1 frankfurter, sliced

In a 2-quart saucepan gradually stir milk into soup. Heat to boiling. Remove from heat and stir in cheese until melted. If necessary, return to low heat to finish melting cheese. (Do not boil.) Garnish with slices of frankfurter and additonal bits of cheese. Yield: 4 cups.

SAUCY LUNCHEON MEAT

6 servings
2 packages (3 ounces each) cream cheese
1/4 cup finely chopped onion
2 tablespoons sliced ripe olives
3/4 cup canned condensed cream of mushroom soup
2 tablespoons milk
1 pound bologna or other luncheon meat,
    finely diced
2 teaspoons prepared mustard
Biscuits, cooked rice, or noodles

Blend cream cheese with milk in top of double broiler. Add meat, onion, olives, mustard and soup; mix thoroughly. Heat over simmering water 15 to 20 minutes, stirring occasionally. Serve over biscuits, rice, or noodles.

FISH

We have drawn together a few specially selected recipes featuring halibut, salmon, tuna and Alaska king crab. For those who enjoy seafood, these selections should be most appealing!!!

VEGETABLE STUFFED HALIBUT

2 large halibut steaks
   (approximately 2 pounds)
1/3 cup chopped onion
1 stalk celery, diced
1/4 pound fresh mushrooms, sliced
1 carrot, grated
1½ tablespoons butter
2 tablespoons water

1 tablespoon chopped parsley
2 teaspoons lemon juice
½ teaspoon salt
½ teaspoon rosemary
Salt and pepper
2 slices bacon, diced
Parsley and lemon slices, for garnish

Thaw frozen halibut. Simmer onion, celery, mushrooms and carrot in covered saucepan with butter and water for 5 minutes. Add parsley, lemon juice, ½ teaspoon salt and rosemary. Mix thoroughly. Season halibut steaks with salt and pepper. Place one halibut steak in oiled baking pan. Cover with vegetable stuffing and the second steak. Sprinkle with chopped bacon. Bake at 375 degrees F. approximately 20 to 25 minutes, or until halibut flakes when tested with a fork. Garnish with parsley and lemon slices. Makes 6 servings.

HALIBUT MEDITERRANEAN

2½ to 3 pounds halibut steaks,
   fresh or frozen
4 medium potatoes, cooked
Salt and pepper
½ cup finely chopped onion
1/3 cup chopped green pepper
2 cloves garlic, minced
2 tablespoons olive oil

2 tomatoes, seeded and diced
1 tablespoon lemon juice
2 tablespoons chopped parsley
1 teaspoon salt
1/4 teaspoon freshly
   ground pepper
1/4 teaspoon thyme

If halibut is frozen, defrost in refrigerator. Peel and slice potatoes 1/4 inch thick. Arrange potatoes in shallow buttered baking dish. Sprinkle with salt and pepper. Arrange halibut steaks in single layer over potatoes. Saute' onion, green pepper and garlic in olive oil. Add tomatoes and saute' 1 minute. Add remaining ingredients. Spoon over halibut steaks. Bake in a 375 degree F. oven 20 minutes or until halibut is fork-tender. Test for doneness by flaking with a fork.
Makes 6 servings.

11

KING CRAB SUPPER DISH TAILORED FOR TWO

1-7½ ounce can Alaska King Crab or
  1-6 ounce package frozen Alaska King Crab
½ pound fresh zucchini
2 tablespoons butter
½ cup chicken bouillon
2 teaspoons lemon juice
1/4 teaspoon salt
1/8 teaspoon pepper

1/4 teaspoon oregano
2 tablespoons cream
2 tablespoons minced parsley
2 tablespoons grated Parmesan cheese
4 ounces noodles or spaghetti,
  cooked and drained
Tomato wedges and parsley, for garnish

Drain and slice canned crab. Or defrost, drain and slice frozen crab. Thinly slice zucchini. Saute' zucchini slowly in butter until nearly tender. Add crab, bouillon, lemon juice and seasonings. Cover and simmer 3 minutes. Add cream, parsley and Parmesan cheese. Toss crab and zucchini mixture with hot cooked noodles or spaghetti. Garnish with tomato wedges and parsley. Makes 2 servings.

12

BAKED STUFFED FISH

1 dressed fish (3 pounds), fresh or frozen
2 tablespoons melted fat or oil
Salt and pepper, as desired
3 cups stuffing

Thaw frozen fish. Clean, wash, and dry fish. Sprinkle inside with salt and pepper. Place fish on a well-greased 18x13 inch bake-and-serve platter. Stuff fish loosely. Brush fish with fat. Bake at 350° F. (moderate oven) 45 to 60 minutes, or until the fish flakes easily when tested with a fork. Note: Fish may be baked without stuffing. 6 servings.

SALMON LOAF

1 can (16 ounces) salmon
3 cups soft breadcrumbs
1/3 cup salmon liquid
2 tablespoons finely chopped green pepper
1/8 teaspoon pepper
½ cup milk
1/4 cup butter or margarine, melted
3 egg yolks, beaten
2 tablespoons finely chopped onion
1 tablespoon lemon juice
3 egg whites, stiffly beaten

Drain salmon; save the liquid. Flake salmon. Heat milk. Add breadcrumbs and butter or margarine and let stand 5 minutes. Add salmon liquid and beat until smooth. Add egg yolks, green pepper, onion, lemon juice, pepper, and salmon; mix well. Fold in egg whites. Pour into a well-greased 1-½ quart loafpan. Bake at 350°F. 40 to 50 minutes, or until firm in center. Remove from oven and let stand 5 minutes. Loosen from sides of pan with a spatula and invert on a serving platter. Serve plain or with a sauce. 6 servings.

TOPSY TURVY TUNA PIE

1 can (6-½ or 7 ounces) tuna
1 tablespoon tuna oil
2 eggs, beaten
½ cup soft breadcrumbs
1 package (12 ounces) cornbread or corn muffin mix
2 tablespoons chopped onion
1 can (10-½ ounces) condensed cream of mushroom soup
6 thin slices lemon or orange

Drain tuna; save oil. Flake tuna. Cook onion in oil until tender. Add soup, eggs, breadcrumbs, and tuna; mix well. Arrange lemon or orange slices on the bottom of a well-greased 10-inch piepan. Pour tuna mixture over fruit slices. Prepare cornbread mix as directed on package. Spreak batter over tuna mixture. Bake at 400°F. 25 to 30 minutes, or until brown. Remove from oven and let stand 5 minutes. Loosen from sides of pan with a spatula and invert on a serving plate. 6 servings.

STUFFED KING CRAB LEGS

3 packages (12 ounces each) precooked, frozen king crab legs
1 can (4 ounces) mushroom stems and pieces, drained
2 tablespoons melted fat or oil
2 tablespoons flour
½ teaspoon salt
1 cup milk
½ cup grated cheese
Paprika

Thaw frozen crab legs. Remove meat from shells. Remove any cartilage and cut meat into ½-inch pieces. Cook mushrooms in fat for 5 minutes. Blend in flour and salt. Add milk gradually and cook until thick, stirring constantly. Add cheese and crab meat; heat. Fill shells with crab mixture. Sprinkle with paprika. Place stuffed crab legs on a grill, shell side down, about 4 inches from moderately hot coals. Heat for 10 to 12 minutes. Serves 6.

FISHERMAN'S DELIGHT

2 pounds pan-dressed yellow perch or other small fish, fresh or frozen
2 tablespoons lemon juice
2 teaspoons salt
1/4 teaspoon pepper
1 pound sliced bacon

Thaw frozen fish. Clean, wash, and dry fish. Brush inside of fish with lemon juice and sprinkle with salt and pepper. Wrap each fish with a slice of bacon. Place fish in well-greased, hinged wire grills. Cook about 5 inches from moderately hot coals for 10 minutes. Turn and cook for 10 to 15 minutes longer or until bacon is crisp and fish flakes easily when tested with a fork. Serves 6.

ZESTY LAKE TROUT

2 pounds lake trout fillets or other fish fillets, fresh or frozen
1/4 cup French dressing
1 tablespoon lemon juice
1 tablespoon grated onion
2 teaspoons salt
Dash pepper

Thaw frozen fillets. Cut into serving-size portions and place in well-greased, hinged wire grills. Combine remaining ingredients. Baste fish with sauce. Cook about 4 inches from moderately hot coals for 8 minutes. Baste with sauce. Turn and cook for 7 to 10 minutes longer or until fish flakes easily when tested with fork. Serves 6.

MEATS

Most of us Americans are hearty meat and potato lovers. We offer an interesting collection of favorites, from fabulous steak to the lowly and less expensive hamburger, with some easy ground meat dishes sandwiched in between. With the broiled sirloin steak we have entered a special Hashed Brown Potato recipe which makes a great meal with a green salad, or Fettucini Alfredo, an Italian Parmesan cheese-noodle dish, which may be served instead of potatoes for a delightful change. Equally at home with steak and a green salad. Several pork, ham and a few lamb dishes are offered. ENJOY!!!

BEEF STUFFED GREEN PEPPERS

1½ pounds ground beef
3 green peppers, cut in half lengthwise
1/3 cup uncooked oats
1/3 cup catsup
1/4 cup finely chopped onion
1 egg, beaten
1 tablespoon Worcestershire sauce
1 teaspoon salt
1/8 teaspoon pepper
1/4 cup catsup

Remove seeds and membrane from green pepper halves and cook in boiling salted water 3 minutes. Invert and drain throughly. Combine oats, catsup, onion, egg, Worcestershire sauce, salt and pepper. Add to ground beef mixing lightly but thoroughly. Pack approximately ½ cup meat mixture into each pepper half. Place peppers in a 12x8-inch baking dish; top meat mixture in each with 2 teaspoons catsup. Bake in a moderate oven (350°F.) 30-35 minutes. 6 servings.

BEEF RIB EYE ROAST

Place a 4 to 10-pound beef rib eye (Delmonico) roast, fat side up, on rack in open roasting pan. Insert meat thermometer so the bulb reaches the center of the thickest part, being sure it does not rest in fat. Do not add water. Do not cover. Roast in a moderate oven (325°F.) to the desired degree of doneness. The meat thermometer will register 140°F. for rare; 160°F. for medium; 170°F. for well done. For roast weighing 4 to 6 pounds, allow 18 to 20 minutes per pound for rare; 20 to 22 minutes for medium; 22 to 24 for well done. For a 7 to 10-pound roast allow 15 to 17 minutes per pound for rare; 17 to 19 for medium; 19 to 21 for well done. Allow to stand in a warm place 15 to 20 minutes before carving. Since roasts usually continue to cook during this time, it is best to remove them from the oven when the thermometer registers about 5°F. below the temperature of doneness desired.

SPECIAL STUFFED POTATOES

6 to 8 baking potatoes
½ cup diced green pepper
1/4 cup butter or margarine
½ to 2/3 cup hot milk
1 ½ to 2 teaspoons salt
1/8 teaspoon pepper
1/4 cup shredded Cheddar cheese

Scrub potatoes, prick each with a fork and wrap individually in Reynolds Wrap and bake in hot oven (400°F.)* until done, approximately 1 hour. Cut slice from top of each potato immediately and scoop out centers, being careful not to break skins. Cook green pepper in butter or margarine for 2 to 3 minutes; remove green pepper and reserve. Mash potatoes; add the butter or margarine, hot milk, salt and pepper and beat until light. Fold in reserved green pepper and fill potato shells with the mixture; return to foil wrappings, folding foil to make containers. Sprinkle shredded cheese on top. Return to oven and bake 15 minutes. Serves 6 to 8.
*Or bake with roast at 325°F. until done, approximately 2 hours.

BROILED SIRLOIN STEAK

(Pictured, Page 16)

1 beef sirloin steak, cut 1 to 2 inches thick
Salt
Pepper

Place steak on grill over ash-covered coals so the top of 1-inch steak is 2 to 3 inches from the heat and 2-inch steak is 3 to 5 inches from the heat. Broil at moderate temperature. When one side is browned, season, turn and finish cooking on the second side. Season. Steaks cut 1 inch thick require 18 to 20 minutes for rare and 20 to 25 minutes for medium. Steaks cut 2 inches thick require 30 to 40 minutes for rare and 35 to 45 minutes for medium

HASHED BROWN POTATOES

Blend together 1/4 cup flour, 1/3 cup milk, 1 teaspoon salt and 1/4 teaspoon pepper. Add to 4 cups cold, cooked and finely grated or chopped potatoes. Mix well. Preheat electric skillet to 340 degrees F. Heat 1/4 cup bacon fat (if you like it) or oil, and add 2/3 cup chopped onion and cook 3 to 5 minutes, until soft but not brown. Lift onions from pan into potato mixture, and mix well. Turn potato mixture into pan, adding more fat if necessary. Spread evenly over pan with a spatula and cook about 20 minutes or until crisp and brown. Turn to brown other side. Makes 6 servings.

FETTUCINI ALFREDO

½ pound fettucini noodles
Chopped parsley
½ to 3/4 cup freshly grated parmesan cheese
1 stick butter or margarine (1/4 pound)
½ pint heavy cream

Cook noodles until slightly crunchy. Rinse in cold water. Melt butter, put ½ aside in cup. Heat ½ cream and ½ butter until bubbly. Add noodles and parsley. Toss gently until cream starts to cook off. Add rest of butter and cream, then as you toss, add as much cheese as desired. Grind Fresh pepper liberally and serve. Serves 4-6 portions.

BEEF STROGANOFF

1/3 cup flour
1/4 teaspoon pepper
½ cup finely chopped onion
1/4 cup fat or oil
1 can (8 ounces) sliced mushrooms, drained
Cooked rice
1 teaspoon salt
1 pound sirloin tip steak, cut in very
    thin strips
1 can (10½ ounces) condensed
    cream of mushroom soup
1 cup sour cream
paprika, parsley

Combine flour, salt and pepper. Coat meat strips with flour mixture. Brown meat in hot fat in a large frypan. Add onion and cook until clear. Drain off excess fat. Add soup and mushrooms. Simmer, covered, 10 to 15 minutes. Blend in sour cream and remove from heat. Serve over rice. Sprinkle with paprika and garnish with parsley. 6 servings.

SWISS STEAK

2 pounds beef chuck about ½" thick
1/4 cup flour
1/8 teaspoon pepper
16 ounce can tomatoes
1 medium onion, sliced
meat tenderizer
salt as desired
2 tablespoons fat or oil
1 stalk celery, diced

Cut meat into six servings, if desired. Treat meat with tenderizer. Mix flour and seasonings; coat meat with mixture. Heat fat in a large frypan. Brown meat on both sides in frypan, turning once. Drain off fat.
Add remaining ingredients. Cover tightly and simmer until meat is tender about 1-½ to 1-3/4 hours.

MEATBALL AND RICE CASSEROLE

6 servings (1 cup each)
1 pound ground beef
1/4 cup milk, whole or skim
1 teaspoon salt
2 tablespoons fat or oil, if desired
½ cup celery, thinly sliced
10½ ounce can cream of mushroom soup,
    condensed, canned
Paprika, as desired
½ cup fine dry breadcrumbs
2 tablespoons onion, chopped
1 teaspoon worcestershire sauce
2 cups rice, cooked
½ cup green pepper, finely chopped
1/3 cup water
½ cup cheddar cheese, shredded
Parsley, if desired

Combine ground beef, breadcrumbs, milk, onion, salt, and worcestershire sauce. Shape into 18 meatballs about 1½ inches in diameter. Brown meatballs in fat, if desired, or in an ungreased fry pan. Preheat oven to 350°F. Place meatballs in a 2-quart casserole. Mix rice, celery, green pepper, soup and water. Pour mixture over meatballs. Bake 40 to 45 minutes. Top with shredded cheese, if desired. Bake 5 minutes longer, or until cheese is melted and lightly browned. Sprinkle with paprika. Garnish with parsley, if desired.

GROUND BEEF CHOP SUEY

6 servings, 3/4 cup chop suey and 2/3 cup rice each
2 cups celery, thin 1" strips
1 pound ground beef
2 tablespoons cornstarch
1 beef bouillon cube
½ teaspoon salt
4 cups rice, cooked (about 1-1/3 cups uncooked)
½ cup onion, sliced
1 tablespoon fat or oil
1½ cups water
1/4 cup soy sauce
4 cups cabbage, chopped

Cook celery, onion, and ground beef in hot fat in a large frypan about 5 minutes until meat begins to brown. Blend cornstarch with water and stir into beef mixture. Add bouillon cube, soy sauce, and salt. Cook stirring constantly. until sauce is thickened and clear. Stir in cabbage. Cook, covered, about 3 minutes until cabbage is tender but still firm. Serve on rice.

BEEF CURRY IN A HURRY WITH CHEESE CORN BREAD TOPPER

(Pictured Page 19)

3 tablespoons butter
½ cup chopped onion
1 clove garlic, minced
1½ pounds boneless beef, cut in ½ inch cubes
1½ cups water
1 to 1½ tablespoons curry powder
1 teaspoon salt
½ cup golden raisins
1/4 cup water
1 tablespoon all-purpose flour
1 medium apple, peeled, sliced
1 package (10 ounce.) frozen peas and carrots,
    thawed
1 package (10 ounce) corn bread mix
1 cup (4 ounce) cubed Cheddar cheese

Melt butter in a large skillet over medium heat; saute' onion and garlic until tender. Add meat and brown. Blend curry powder and salt into 1½ cups water; add to skillet along with raisins. Cover and simmer 20 minutes or until meat is tender. Blend flour in 1/4 cup water until smooth. Gradually stir into meat mixture. Bring to boiling point, stirring constantly. Add apple. Turn into 2-quart casserole. Arrange peas and carrots over meat mixture. Prepare corn bread according to package directions. Fold Cheddar cheese cubes into batter. Spread over top of casserole or arrange batter to make stripes across casserole. Bake in preheated 425 degree oven, 12-15 minutes. Makes 8 servings.

MEAT LOAF

6 servings, 2 slices each
1½ pounds ground beef, regular
1/3 cup onion, finely chopped
3 tablespoons parsley, chopped
3/4 cup milk, whole or skim or
    3/4 cup cooked tomatoes
1/8 teaspoon pepper
1/4 pound fresh pork sausage, bulk
3 tablespoons celery, finely chopped
3/4 cup breadcrumbs, soft
1 egg beaten   3/4 teaspoon salt

Preheat oven to 350° F. (moderate). Blend all ingredients thoroughly. Pack mixture into a 9-by 5-by 3-inch loaf pan. Bake 1-½ hours.

CANTONESE BEEF

2 pounds beef for stew,
   cut in 1 1/4 inch pieces
2 tablespoons cooking fat
½ teaspoon salt
½ teaspoon ginger
1 medium onion, chopped
1½ cups water
3 tablespoons soy sauce

2 tablespoons cornstarch
2 cups sliced celery
½ pound mushrooms, sliced
1 small green pepper, cut in strips
1 can (8 ounces) water chestnuts,
   drained
1 can (16 ounces) mandarin orange
   segments, drained

Brown meat in hot cooking fat in large frying pan. Pour off drippings. Sprinkle salt and ginger over meat; add onion, 1 cup water and soy sauce and heat to boiling. Reduce heat, cover tightly and cook slowly 1½ hours or until meat is tender. Blend ½ cup water with cornstarch, stir into meat mixture and cook, stirring constantly until mixture thickens. Stir in celery, mushrooms, green pepper and water chestnuts and continue cooking, covered, 5 to 7 minutes. Fold in mandarin orange segments. Serve with chow mein noodles or cooked rice. 6 to 8 servings.

CHINESE PEPPER STEAK

1 1/4 pounds top round steak,
   cut 3/4 to 1 inch thick***
1 tablespoon cornstarch
½ teaspoon sugar
1/4 teaspoon ginger
1/4 cup soy sauce

3 medium green peppers
3 small tomatoes
2 tablespoons cooking oil
1 clove garlic, minced
1/4 cup water

Partially freeze steak to firm and slice diagonally across the grain into very thin strips. Combine cornstarch, sugar and ginger and stir in soy sauce. Pour mixture over meat and stir. Cut green peppers into thin strips (½ inch) and cut tomatoes into wedges. Quickly brown beef strips (1/3 at a time) in hot oil and remove from pan. Reduce heat add green pepper, garlic and water to pan and cook until pepper is tender crisp, 5 to 6 minutes. Stir in meat and tomatoes and heat through. 4 servings. ings.
***1 flank steak (approximately 1 1/4 pounds) may be used instead of top round. If you want to splurge, try a sirloin steak slice. Delicious!!!

FLANK STEAK A LA BLUE

Shallow dish
1/3 cup white wine vinegar
1/3 cup water
2 tablespoons soy sauce
1 medium onion, sliced

1 clove garlic, sliced
Freshly ground pepper
1½ to 2 pounds flank steak, scored
1/4 cup Blue cheese, crumbled

In shallow dish prepare marinade by combining vinegar, water, soy sauce, onion, garlic and pepper. Marinate steak at least 6 hours, turning occasionally. Place steak 4-5 inches from coals or if broiling in broiler, 4-5 inches from heat. Broil 5-7 minutes. Turn and sprinkle with Blue cheese. Continue to broil to desired degree of doneness. Place on serving platter. Slice in thin diagonal slices across grain.

BEEF PATTY DUO

2 pounds ground beef
2 teaspoons salt
1/8 teaspoon pepper
Yogurt
Bleu Cheese
Corn relish

Combine Ground beef, salt and pepper and shape into 6 to 8 patties ½ to 3/4 inch thick. Place on rack in broiler pan so surface of meat is 3 to 4 inches from heat. Broil 5 to 7 minutes, turn and broil 5 to 8 minutes, to desired doneness. Meanwhile, combine yogurt with crumbled bleu cheese. Top half the patties with yogurt mixture and half with corn relish. 6 to 8 patties.

GO-FURTHER HAMBURGERS

1 egg, slightly beaten
3 slices bread, cubed or crumbs
1 teaspoon Worcestershire sauce
1/4 teaspoon pepper
1 tablespoon fat
1/3 cup water
1/4 cup onion, finely chopped
1 teaspoon salt
1 pound ground beef

Mix ingredients except beef and fat. Add beef and mix thoroughly. Shape into 12 thin or 6 thick burgers. Heat fat in a heavy frypan over moderate heat. Brown burgers on both sides, turning once. Reduce heat and continue cooking, if needed, until meat is no longer pink when a knife is inserted into the center. Thin burgers take about 8 minutes total cooking time and thick ones, about 16 minutes.

MEXICAN CHEESEBURGERS

1 pound ground beef, chuck or round
1 green pepper, chopped
1 onion, chopped
1 can tomato soup
Salt and pepper to taste
Cayenne red pepper, if desired
Slices of sharp cheddar cheese

Fry green pepper and onion in small amount of oil until soft. Add ground beef, cook until brown. Add tomato soup and seasonings. Remove as much fat as possible before adding soup. Serve on warm hamburger buns with one slice of cheese. Makes 9 sandwiches.

CARROT COINS BEEF LOAF

2 pounds ground beef
  (80 percent lean)
5 long carrots
1 can (16 ounces tomatoes)
1 3/4 teaspoons salt
1 1/8 teaspoon leaf oregano
1/4 teaspoons pepper
1 tablespoon cornstarch

½ cup crushed crackers
2 medium onions, cut in 1/4 inch slices
1 egg
1 small green pepper,
  cut in thin strips
1 cup sliced celery
½ cup water

Cook carrots (whole) in boiling salted water in large covered frying-pan 15 minutes; drain. Drain tomatoes, reserving juice; tomatoes into large pieces. Stir 3/4 cup of reserved tomato juice, 1½ teaspoons salt, 1 teaspoon oregano and pepper into cracker crumbs in large bowl. Chop enough onion slices to make 1/4 cup. Add ground beef, chopped onion and egg to cracker crumb mixture; mix lightly but thoroughly. Place 1/3 of mixture in 9x5-inch loaf pan, pressing into layer in bottom of pan. Place 2 carrots lengthwise in pan and press into meat mixture. Top with layer of second 1/3 of meat mixture. Place 1 carrot down the center and press into meat. Add remaining meat mixture to form layer and press last 2 carrots into top, covering them with meat. Bake in a moderate oven (350°F.) for 1 hour 15 minutes or until done. For vegetable sauce, add remaining onion slices, green pepper, celery, 1/4 teaspoon salt and 1/8 teaspoon oregano to boiling water in saucepan. Cover tightly and cook 15 minutes or until vegetables are almost tender. Combine cornstarch with remaining reserved tomato juice and pieces of tomatoes. Gradually combine with vegetables and cook 3 to 5 minutes, stirring until thickened. Slice meat loaf in 12 equal slices and serve with vegetable sauce. 6 servings of 2 slices each.

STEAK STRIPS IN GRAVY

6 servings
1-½ pounds beef steak, chuck or round,
   about ½ inch thick
1 tablespoon butter or margarine
2-½ cups water, hot
Few drops worcestershire sauce
1 tablespoon tomato puree
1/8 teaspoon pepper
1/3 cup onion, chopped
2 tablespoons fat or oil
3 tablespoons flour
1 teaspoon mustard, prepared
3 tablespoons sour cream
1 teaspoon salt

Cut steak into strips about 3 inches long and 1 inch wide. Brown steak and onion in fat in an ovenproof fry pan. Remove from heat. Preheat oven to 350 degrees F. (moderate). Melt butter or margarine in a 1-quart saucepan. Stir in flour. Add water slowly, stirring constantly. Stir in mustard, worcestershire sauce, sour cream, tomato puree, salt, and pepper. Cook until thickened, stirring constantly. Pour over steak strips. Cover. Bake 2-½ hours or until meat is tender.

QUICK BEEF PIE

6 servings
1-½ pounds ground beef
½ teaspoon salt
1 can (16 ounces) cut green beans, drained
1-½ cups seasoned mashed potatoes
1 medium onion, chopped
1 can (10-½ ounces) condensed tomato soup
1/4 teaspoon pepper
½ cup shredded Cheddar cheese

Crumble beef into large frypan. Add onion and salt, and cook until browned. Drain off excess fat. Add soup, green beans, and pepper; simmer 5 minutes. Pour into greased 2-quart casserole. Drop potatoes in mounds onto hot meat mixture. Sprinkle with cheese. Bake at 350 degrees for 20 minutes.

HAM PATTIES

6 servings
2 cups ground cooked ham
1 tablespoon chopped onion
1/4 teaspoon salt
1 egg, beaten
3 tablespoons fat or oil
1 cup mashed potatoes
1/4 teaspoon dry mustard
1 tablespoon milk
½ cup fine dry breadcrumbs

Combine ground ham, mashed potatoes, onion, mustard, and 1/4 teaspoon salt. Chill about 1 hour. Shape into 12 patties. Blend milk into beaten egg. Dip patties in egg mixture and then in crumbs. Fry patties in hot fat until golden brown.

BARBECUED SHORT RIBS

Pictured

3 pounds beef short ribs
½ cup water
1 cup catchup
½ cup finely chopped onion
1/4 cup vinegar
1/4 cup Worcestershire sauce
2 tablespoons honey
1 tablespoon prepared mustard
1/2 cup water

Add ½ cup water to short ribs. Cover tightly and cook slowly 2 to 2½ hours, or until tender. Combine catchup, onion, vinegar, Worcestershire sauce, honey and mustard for barbecue sauce. When short ribs are tender, remove from liquid and place on rack in broiler pan. Set regulator for broiling. Brush short ribs with barbecue sauce. Insert broiler pan and rack so top of meat is 3 to 4 inches from heat. Broil about 5 minutes. When first side is browned, turn and brush second side with barbecue sauce. Continue broiling second side 2 to 3 minutes. Add ½ cup water to remaining barbecue sauce. Cook slowly 5 to 10 minutes or until flavors are blended. Serve short ribs and sauce on cooked rice. 4 servings.

PEACHY BEEF PINWHEEL

2 pounds ground beef
1 can (16 ounces) sliced cling peaches
1-½ cups soft bread crumbs
2 eggs
1 small onion, finely chopped
1/4 teaspoon nutmeg

2 teaspoons dill weed
2 teaspoons salt
1/4 teaspoon pepper
1 cup cooked rice
1 tablespoon snipped parsley

Drain peaches, reserving syrup, and cut slices in half crosswise. Combine ground beef, bread crumbs, eggs, onion, 1/3 cup reserved syrup, dill weed, salt and pepper. Combine rice, parsley and 1 tablespoon reserved syrup. Pat out meat mixture on waxed paper into a 14x10-inch rectangle, 1/2 to 3/4 inch thick. Spread rice mixture evenly over meat. Stir nutmeg into peaches and place over meat, distributing evenly. Roll up meat mixture from short side of rectangle (jelly-roll fashion) to enclose peaches and form a pinwheel loaf. Press meat over filling at both ends of loaf and place, seam side down, on rack in roasting pan. Bake in moderate oven (350 degrees F.) for 1 hour. Brush with reserved peach juice and continue baking 15 minutes. Let stand 10 minutes before slicing. 8 servings.

MARINATED BEEF KABOBS

2 pounds beef tip, cut in
   1x1½x1½ inch pieces
1/4 cup lemon juice
½ cup chopped onion
2 teaspoons dry mustard
1 teaspoon garlic salt
1 teaspoon salt
1/4 teaspoon pepper
1 cup salad oil
2 small tomatoes
4 sweet pickles
12 small cooked onions

Combine lemon juice, onion, mustard, garlic salt, salt and pepper. Add oil and mix. Place beef cubes and marinade in a plastic bag; tie bag securely and place in pan in refrigerator several hours or overnight. Pour off marinade and reserve. Cut each tomato into 4 to 6 wedges. Cut each pickle in half. Thread cubes of beef on four 12 inch skewers alternately with the vegetables and pickles. Brush with marinade. Place kabobs on grill 3 to 4 inches from heat and broil at moderate temperature, turning and brushing with marinade occasionally, for 12 to 18 minutes, depending upon degree of doneness desired. 6 servings.

CHIPPED BEEF DELUXE

*6 servings, about ½ cup sauce
   and ½ cup noodles each*
2 tablespoons fat or oil
2 tablespoons green pepper, chopped
10-½ ounce can condensed cream of mushroom soup
2 tablespoons pimiento, chopped
3 cups noodles, cooked
½ cup celery, chopped
2 tablespoons onion, chopped
½ cup water
4-ounce package dried beef
2 hard-cooked eggs, diced

Heat fat; add raw vegetables and cook until they begin to brown. Stir mushroom soup, water, and beef into vegetables. Cook, stirring as needed, until thickened. Add pimiento and eggs. Serve on noodles.

NEW WORLD BEEF POT-ROAST

3-½ to 4-pound beef blade roast
1/4 cup flour
1-½ teaspoons salt
1/4 teaspoon pepper
2 tablespoons cooking fat
½ teaspoon anise seed
1 clove garlic, crushed
1 beef bouillon cube
1/3 cup hot water
1 medium onion, chopped
1 can (16 ounces) whole tomatoes
1 can (14-½ ounces) artichoke hearts,
   drained and halved*
1 can (approximately 6 ounces) California pitted
   ripe olives, drained
1/4 cup cold water

Combine flour, salt and pepper; dredge meat. Reserve excess flour. Brown meat in cooking fat in large frying-pan. Pour off drippings. Sprinkle anise seed over meat and add garlic. Crush bouillon cube and dissolve in hot water; add to meat. Cover tightly and cook slowly 1-1/4 hours. Turn meat. Add onion. Drain tomatoes; reserve liquid and add to meat. Continue cooking slowly, covered 1 hour or until meat is tender. Add tomatoes, artichoke hearts and olives and continue cooking 5 to 10 minutes. Remove meat, vegetables and olives to warm platter. Thicken cooking liquid with reserved flour blended with cold water. Serve gravy with meat.
*2 packages (9 ounces each) frozen artichoke hearts, defrosted , may be substituted.

27

CONFETTI BEEF STEW

Pictured

2 pounds beef for stew,
    cut in 1-½-inch pieces
2 Tablespoons cooking fat
1 beef bouillon cube
1 cup hot water
1 teaspoon onion salt
½ teaspoon salt
1/8 teaspoon pepper
1 bay leaf
1 package (10 ounces) frozen peas
1 can (4 ounces) chopped pimiento,
    drained
Flour for thickening, if desired
Cooked rice

Brown beef in cooking fat in Dutch oven. Pour off drippings. Dissolve bouillon cube in water. Add bouillon, onion salt, salt, pepper and bay leaf to beef. Cover tightly and cook slowly 1-½ hours. Add peas and pimiento and continue cooking, covered, 30 minutes or until meat is tender. Thicken with flour, if desired. Serve with cooked rice. 6 servings.

BRUNSWICK STEW

6 servings, 1-½ cups each
3 pounds chicken, whole or cut-up
3 cups water
1-3/4 cups lima beans, frozen
2/3 cup onions, chopped
½ teaspoon salt
1/8 teaspoon poultry seasoning
2 tablespoons flour

1-½ teaspoons salt
1 cup potatoes, diced
16-ounce can tomatoes
1-3/4 cups corn, frozen
1/8 teaspoon pepper
1/4 cup water

Simmer chicken in salted water until tender. Drain off the broth. Separate the meat from the skin and bones and cut meat into pieces as desired. Skim the fat from the broth. Add potatoes to broth and simmer 5 minutes. Add lima beans, tomatoes, and onions. Simmer 7 minutes. Add chicken, corn, and seasonings. Cook 3 minutes longer. Blend 1/4 cup water with flour. Add to stew and heat just long enough to thicken, stirring as needed.

VEAL BIRDS

6 servings, 1 veal bird each
3 slices bacon
1/3 cup celery, chopped
½ cup hot water
2 pounds veal cutlets, thin, boneless
    cut in six serving-size pieces
1 cup beef bouillon
1/4 cup onion, chopped
1-½ cups packaged herb-seasoned
  bread stuffing mix
2 tablespoons flour
2 tablespoons butter or margarine

Fry bacon until crisp; drain on paper and crumble. Cook onion and celery in bacon drippings until tender but not brown. Combine bread stuffing mix, bacon, celery, onion, and bacon drippings; mix well. Add hot water and toss with a fork to mix. Flatten veal cutlets slightly with a mallet if necessary. Place about 1/3 cup stuffing on each piece of veal. Roll up and secure with wooden tooth picks. Roll cutlets in flour. Brown well on all sides in melted butter or margarine. Add bouillon; cover. Simmer 30 to 35 minutes, or until tender. If necessary, add a small amount of hot water during cooking to keep veal birds from sticking.

CALIFORNIA COCIDO

2 to 1-½ pounds beef for stew
3 tablespoons flour
1 teaspoon salt
1 teaspoon paprika
1/4 teaspoon pepper
3 tablespoons cooking fat
1 beef bullion cube
1 cup hot waer
3 medium carrots
½ pound leeks
1 can (15-½ ounces) garbanzo beans
1 clove garlic, crushed
½ pound beef salami
1 can (approximately 6 ounces) California pitted
   ripe olives, drained
1 jar (4 ounces) pimiento, cut in strips
1 teaspoon mint flakes
2 tablespoons water

Combine flour, salt, paprika and pepper; dredge meat and reserve excess flour. Brown meat in cooking fat in large frying pan. Pour off drippings. Crush bouillon cube, dissolve in hot water and add to meat. Cover tightly and cook slowly 1-1/4 hours. Cut carrots in half lengthwise, then crosswise into 2-inch pieces. Cut leeks crosswise into 1-inch pieces. Add beans including liquid, carrots, leeks and garlic to meat and continue cooking, covered, 30 minutes. Cut salami into ½-inch slices; cut each slice into 8 wedges. Add salami, olives, pimiento and mint flakes and continue cooking 10 to 15 minutes. Thicken cooking liquid with reserved flour blended with water. 6 to 8 servings.

PATIO STEAK ROLL-UPS

8 cube steaks, 3½x5 inches (about 2½ lbs.)
Water
1 teaspoon seasoned instant meat tenderizer
8 Cheddar cheese sticks 4x½ inch
8 dill pickles
Melted butter

Moisten both sides of meat with water and sprinkle tenderizer evenly over entire surface. Place a cheese stick and pickle on each steak. Roll and fasten with metal skewers. Place on grill, skewered side down 4-5 inches from coals. Brushing occasionally with butter, grill 4-5 minutes; turn and grill 4-5 additional minutes or until desired degree of doneness. 8 servings.

LONG JOHN SILVER DOGS

1 can (8 ounce) pizza sauce
1/4 cup chopped green onions
8 slices green pepper
16 slices Mozzarella cheese
8 frankfurter buns
   Butter, softened
8 frankfurters

Stir onion into pizza sauce. Cut green pepper in thin strips the length of frankfurter. Cut cheese in slices to fit side of buns. Spread butter on both sides of buns. Split frankfurter lengthwise without cutting through. Using 2 tablespoons sauce for each sandwich, spread a small amount of sauce on cut frank; insert green pepper strip. Spread remaining sauce on both sides of buns. Place slice of cheese on each side of bun and frankfurter in center. Hold together with wooden picks. Wrap in double thickness heavy duty foil. Grill 6 minutes; turn and grill additional 6 minutes or until frankfurter is hot and cheese melts. 8 servings.
Note: Wrapped franks may be refrigerated. Grill about 2 minutes longer on each side.

LAMB STEW

6 servings (1-½ cups each)
1/3 cup flour
1/8 teaspoon pepper
2 tablespoons fat or oil
3-1/4 cups water
4 medium potatoes, cut into 1-inch cubes
1-½ teaspoons salt
1-½ pounds boneless stew lamb, cut into 1-inch cubes
3 medium onions, sliced
5 medium carrots, quartered
1-½ cup peas, frozen

Combine flour, salt, and pepper. Coat lamb with seasoned flour. Brown lamb in moderately hot fat in a dutch oven or deep pot. Sprinkle remaining seasoned flour over browned lamb; stir. Add water and cover tightly. Simmer 1-½ to 2 hours, or until lamb is tender. Add onions, potatoes, and carrots. Simmer, covered, 15 minutes. Add peas, simmer, covered, until vegetables are tender. Stir occasionally.

PORK CHOW MEIN

1-½ pounds pork cubes
½ teaspoon salt
1 large onion, cut in 8
    wedges
½ cup water
1 small head cabbage,
    shredded (8 cups)
1 can (16 ounces) bean
    sprouts, drained
1/3 cup soy sauce
2 tablespoons cornstarch
1/8 teaspoon ginger
Chow mein noodles

Cut pork in ½ to 3/4-inch pieces and brown in large frying-pan. Sprinkle with salt; add onion and water. Cover tightly and cook slowly 45 minutes. Add cabbage and cook 10 minutes. Stir in bean sprouts. Blend soy sauce with cornstarch and ginger and gradually add to pork mixture, stirring to blend. Cook until thickened, stirring occasionally. Serve on chow mein noodles. 6 servings.

JAMAICAN PORK RIBS

4 to 5 pounds pork country style ribs*
1 can (30 ounces) fruit cocktail
2 tablespoons rum
2 tablespoons lime juice
½ teaspoon grated lime peel
½ cup brown sugar
1 teaspoon salt
½ teaspoon garlic powder
½ teaspoon ginger
1/4 teaspoon cloves
1/8 teaspoon pepper
1 bay leaf
Salt and pepper

*Have retailer cut meat into single rib portions or crack the back bone so ribs can be cut apart. Drain fruit cocktail; reserve syrup. Add rum, lime juice and peel to syrup. Combine brown sugar, salt, garlic powder, ginger, cloves and pepper in small saucepan. Stir in reserved syrup and bay leaf; bring to boil and cook slowly 10 minutes. Remove bay leaf and add ½ cup sauce to the fruit cocktail. Place meat on grill, 5 to 7 inches above ash-covered coals, and broil at low to moderate temperature 30 minutes. Turn meat, season with salt and pepper and broil 30 minutes; turn and season. Brush ribs with sauce and continue broiling 30 to 50 minutes, or until meat is done, turning and brushing with sauce occasionally. Heat fruit cocktail 5 minutes, stirring occasionally; serve with meat. 6 to 8 servings. Note: 1 can (30 ounces) sliced cling peaches may be substituted for the fruit cocktail, if desired.

PORK-STUFFED ONIONS

2 pounds ground pork
4 large Idaho-Oregon Sweet Spanish onions
    (3 to 4 inches in diameter)
2 teaspoons salt
3/4 teaspoon dill weed
1/8 teaspoon pepper
1 cup cooked rice
1 can (11 ounces) condensed Cheddar cheese soup
1 egg
1/3 cup diced green pepper
1 tablespoon flour
1/4 cup milk
Thin pimiento strips
2 slices bacon, cut in 1-inch pieces and fried

Peel onions and cut in halves crosswise. Parboil in salted water 5 minutes. Drain. Remove centers of onions, leaving about ½-inch thick shells. Chop enough of the onion centers to measure ½ cup.* Sprinkle salt, dill weed and pepper over ground pork. Add chopped onion, rice, 2/3 cup of the cheese soup, egg and green pepper; stir lightly to combine. Divide mixture into 8 portions and place a portion in each onion cup, rounding the top. Place stuffed onions in roasting pan. Pour 1/4 cup boiling water into pan, cover tightly and bake in moderate oven (350 degrees F.) for 50 minutes. Baste onions with pan liquid and bake, uncovered, 10 minutes or until done. Remove onions to warm platter and keep warm. Pour off all but ½ cup pan liquid; stir in flour to blend. Add milk to remaining soup in can, stirring to mix; add to pan liquid and cook, stirring constantly until blended and thickened. Arrange a pimiento strip in a circle on each onion and fill with pieces of bacon. Serve cheese sauce with the stuffed onions. 8 servings.
*Save remaining centers of onions to use later in stews, soups casseroles or gravies.

SCALLOPED SAUSAGE AND CABBAGE

1-½ pounds pork sausage
    links
2 tablespoons water
1-½ pounds (8 cups)
    finely cut cabbage
1/4 cup butter or
    margarine
1/4 cup flour
1-½ teaspoons salt
2 cups milk
1/4 cup chopped green
    pepper
1 tablespoon butter
    or margarine
½ cup dry bread crumbs

Place sausage links and water in cold fry pan. Cover tightly and cook slowly 5 minutes. Remove cover and lightly brown links. Pour off drippings. Cook cabbage in boiling, salted water 5 minutes and drain. Melt 1/4 cup butter or margarine and blend in flour and salt. Gradually add milk and cook, stirring constantly until thickened. Add green pepper. Place half the cabbage in the bottom of casserole and arrange half of the sausage links on top of cabbage. Pour over half of the sauce mixture. Add remaining cabbage and sauce; top with sausage links. Melt 1 tablespoon butter or margarine and mix with the crumbs. Sprinkle crumbs around edge of casserole. Bake in moderate oven (350 degrees F.) 30 minutes. 4 to 6 servings.

CREAMED SAUSAGE ON TOAST

½ pound bulk sausage
2 tablespoons flour
1-½ cups milk

Pan fry bulk sausage, breaking into small pieces with fork. Reduce heat and add flour, mixing thoroughly. Add milk, bring to boil to thicken. Cook 2 to 3 minutes and serve over hot toast. A good breakfast dish.

BUTTERFLY PORK CHOPS

6 to 8 butterfly pork chops,
    cut 3/4 to 1 inch thick
2 tablespoons lard or
    drippings
Salt and pepper
1/4 cup water

Brown the chops in lard or drippings in frying-pan. Pour off drippings. Season with salt and pepper. Add water. Cover tightly and simmer 45 minutes to 1 hour, or until done. 6 to 8 servings.

PORK CHOP ROAST WITH PEAR-CORNBREAD STUFFING

1-½ cups diced Anjou or Bosc pears
½ cup chopped onion
½ cup chopped celery
½ cup butter or margarine
1 (8 ounce) package cornbread stuffing mix
1/4 cup chopped parsley
1/4 cup chopped peanuts

1/4 teaspoon salt
Dash pepper
1/4 teaspoon thyme
1/4 cup hot water
6 (3/4 inch thick) loin pork chops
Fresh Western winter pear wedges and
    cranberry sauce for garnish

Core and dice pears, but do not peel. Saute' onion and celery in butter or margarine. Add stuffing mix, pears, parsley, peanuts and seasonings and mix throughly. Add hot water and toss lightly to moisten. Place stuffing between chops and arrange in baking pan. Run skewers through chops to hold in place. Bake in 350 degree F. oven 1-½ hours. Arrange Pork Chop Roast on platter and garnish with wedges of fresh Western winter pears and cranberry sauce. Makes 6 servings.

PORK STUFFED CABBAGE ROLLS

1½ pounds ground pork
1 medium cabbage
2 quarts boiling water
1½ teaspoons salt
½ teaspoon dill weed
1/8 teaspoon pepper
1 small onion, chopped
1/4 cup finely chopped
  celery
1 egg
1 can (11 ounces) condensed
  Cheddar cheese soup
1 cup cooked rice
1/4 cup boiling water
Flour for gravy, if desired
Paprika, if desired

Cut core from cabbage, place head in saucepan, add boiling water and cook 3 to 4 minutes. Drain cabbage and remove and reserve 12 leaves as they become flexible. Sprinkle salt, dill weed and pepper over ground pork. Add onion, celery, egg and ½ cup of cheese soup; stir lightly to combine. Stir in cooked rice and divide meat mixture into 12 equal parts. Place one portion of meat mixture in each cabbage leaf. Roll leaves and fold ends to enclose filling; place rolls, seam-side down, in large frying pan. (Rolls can be secured with small round wooden picks, if necessary.) Add 1/4 cup water, cover tightly and cook 30 minutes. Add remaining cheese soup and cook, covered, 10 minutes or until cabbage and pork are done. Remove rolls to warm platter; thicken cheese sauce with flour, if desired, and serve over rolls. Sprinkle with paprika, if desired. 6 servings of 2 rolls each.

SWEET-SOUR PORK

6 servings, 2/3 cup sauce and ½ cup rice each
2-½ cups pork shoulder, lean,
  1" pieces (1-1/4 pounds)
1/8 teaspoon pepper
1½ cups green pepper, 1" pieces
3 tablespoons cornstarch
1/3 cup vinegar
3 cups rice cooked (1 cup uncooked)
2 tablespoons fat or oil
1 teaspoon garlic salt
1-3/4 cups water
½ cup raisins
1/3 cup sugar
1/4 cup soy sauce

Brown meat in hot fat or oil. Add garlic salt, pepper, and water. Cover and simmer about 40 minutes until meat is tender. Add green pepper and continue cooking until it is tender. Mix remaining ingredients, except rice, and stir into meat mixture. Cook, uncovered, until broth is clear and thickened. Stir just enough to prevent sticking. Serve on rice.

SPICY POT ROAST

10 to 15 servings
1/4 cup vinegar
3 cloves, whole
3/4 teaspoon salt
3 to 5 pounds beef round roast
1 cup water
1 bay leaf
3/4 teaspoon sugar

Combine ingredients and pour over beef. Let stand 14 hours in the refrigerator. Place meat and liquid in a heavy pot or Dutch oven; cover. Simmer over low heat until tender, or bake at 350°F. (moderate oven) for about 2½ hours. Serve the hot liquid with the roast.

MEATS

GLAZED BAKED HAM—
TASTY BACON GARNISH

7 to 10-pound canned ham
½ cup apple jelly
1 jar (10 ounces) sweet pickled watermelon rind
1 teaspoon lemon juice
12 to 16 slices bacon

Place ham on a rack in an open roasting pan. Insert roast meat thermometer so the bulb is centered in the thickest part. Do not add water. Do not cover. Roast in a slow oven (325 degrees F.) until meat thermometer registers 130 degrees F. Combine apple jelly with 1 tablespoon of syrup from watermelon rind and lemon juice in small sauce pan. Cook slowly, stirring until smooth. Brush warm glaze over ham and return to oven until thermometer registers 140 degrees F. Allow approximately 15 to 18 minutes per pound. Remove ham and turn oven up to hot (400 degrees F.)*. Place bacon slices on rack in a pan (broiler pan may be used.) Bake for 15 minutes (until almost done.) Immediately wrap each bacon slice around a piece of watermelon rind, securing with small wooden pick, and bake 2 to 4 minutes.
*Bacon can be baked in oven with the ham at 325 degrees F. for 20 to 25 minutes before wrapping around rind.
Note: To decorate ham, arrange canned apricot halves, maraschino cherries, slivers of lemon peel and strips of green onion on top of glazed ham to form flowers 5 minutes before end of cooking time. Brush fruit and stems with glaze and return to oven.

TIME TABLE FOR HAMS

(Roasted at 325 degrees F. Oven Temperature)

Type and Style	Weight	Approximate Total Cooking Time
Canned Hams	1-½ to 3 lbs.	1 to 1-½ hrs.
	3 to 7 lbs.	1-½ to 2 hrs.
	7 to 10 lbs.	2 to 2-½ hrs.
Boneless Ham, Fully-Cooked	3 to 5 lbs. (half)	1-½ to 1-3/4 hrs.
	7 to 10 lbs.	2-½ to 3 hrs.
	10 to 12 lbs.	3 to 3-½ hrs.
Bone-In Ham, Fully-Cooked	3 to 4 lbs. (portion)	1-½ to 1-3/4 hrs.
	5 to 7 lbs. (half)	2 to 2-¼ hrs.
	10 to 13 lbs.	3 to 3-½ hrs.
	13 to 16 lbs.	3-½ to 4 hrs.
Semi-Boneless Ham, Fully-Cooked	4 to 6 lbs. (half)	1-3/4 to 2-½ hrs.
	10 to 12 lbs.	3 to 3-½ hrs.
Bone-In Ham, Cook-Before-Eating	3 to 4 lbs. (portion)	2-½ to 2-3/4 hrs.
	5 to 7 lbs. (half)	3 to 3-1/4 hrs.
	10 to 12 lbs.	3-½ to 4 hrs.
	12 to 15 lbs.	4 to 4-½ hrs.

BAKED SMOKED HALF HAM

Pictured, Page 35

5 to 7-pound smoked half ham
(shank* or butt)

Place ham, fat side up, on rack in an open roasting pan. Insert meat thermometer so the bulb is centered in the thickest part. Be careful that bulb does not rest in fat or on bone. Do not add water. Do not cover. Roast in a slow oven (325 degrees F.) until the meat thermometer registers 140 degrees F. for a "fully-cooked" half ham. (18 to 24 minutes per pound); 160 degrees F. for a "cook-before-eating" half ham (22 to 25 minutes per pound).
*Have retailer remove piece from end of shank (1 to 1-½ pounds) for Ham and Bean Soup, if desired.

HAM LOAF

1 pound lean ground ham
1 pound lean ground pork
1 cup corn flakes
2 eggs beaten
1 cup milk
1 teaspoon salt
1 teaspoon pepper

Mix together. Pack in loaf pan, pull meat away from sides with scraper. Bake 350 degrees F. for 30 minutes then 250 degrees F. for 1-½ hours.

Baste with sauce:
½ cup brown sugar
1/4 cup vinegar
½ cup warm water
1/4 cup Worcestershire sauce
1 teaspoon dry mustard

Combine above five ingredients in a small saucepan. Bring to boil. Baste every fifteen minutes.

SUPER STUFFED PORK CHOPS

6 to 8 pork rib chops, cut 1-1/4 to 1-½ inches thick
1 package (7 ounces) cornbread stuffing mix
1/3 cup honey

1 tablespoon prepared mustard
1 tablespoon lemon juice
Salt and pepper

Make a pocket in each chop by cutting into the chop on rib side parallel to the surface of the chop. Be careful not to cut through the opposite side. Prepare stuffing according to package directions, using amount of water specified for less moist stuffing. Cool. To prepare glaze, combine honey, mustard and lemon juice in small saucepan and cook 5 to 10 minutes to thicken, stirring occasionally. Stuff pocket in each chop with an equal amount of the stuffing mixture. Place chops on grill so surface of meat is 5 to 7 inches from heat and cook at low to moderate temperature 20 minutes, turning occasionally. Season chops on both sides with salt and pepper. Broil 10 to 15 minutes longer, or until chops are done, brushing with glaze and turning occasionally. 6 to 8 servings.

LAMB CROWN ROAST

3-½ to 4 pound lamb crown
  roast
Cooked seasoned mixed
  vegetables, if desired

Have the butcher fashion a lamb crown roast of 14 to 16 ribs. Place crown roast, rib ends down, on rack in an open roasting pan. Do not add water. Do not cover. Roast in a slow oven (325 degrees F.) for 1-1/4 hours. Turn roast so rib ends are up. Insert roast meat thermometer into center of thickest part of roast, being careful the thermometer does not rest on bone or fat. Continue roasting to desired degree of doneness. 140 degrees F. for rare; 160 degrees F. for medium; 170 degrees F. to 180 degrees F. for well done. Allow 30 to 35 minutes per pound total cooking time for rare; 35 to 40 minutes per pound for medium and 40 to 45 minutes per pound for well done. To serve, place paper frills on each rib end and fill crown with cooked mixed vegetables if desired.

LAMB AND VEGETABLE CASSEROLE

6 servings (1 cup each)
10-ounce package lima beans, frozen
1 cup boiling water
2 tablespoons onion, chopped
10-½ ounce can cream of mushroom soup, condensed
1/4 teaspoon thyme
½ teaspoon salt
1-½ cups carrots, thinly sliced
1½ pounds ground lamb
1 tablespoon fat or oil
1/3 cup vegetable liquid
1-½ teaspoons salt
6 tomato slices, 3/4-inch thick
2 tablespoons parmesan cheese, grated

Add lima beans and carrots to boiling water. Cook, covered, until tender, about 15 to 20 minutes. Drain; save cooking liquid. Preheat oven to 350 degrees F. (moderate). Cook ground lamb and onion in fat until lamb is lightly browned and onion is transparent. Pour off drippings. Add soup, vegetable liquid, vegetables, salt, and thyme. Mix well. Pour into a 2-quart casserole. Arrange tomato slices on top of mixture. Sprinkle with salt and cheese. Bake 35 to 40 minutes.

LAMB AND EGGPLANT CASSEROLE

6 servings (1 cup each)
1 medium (about 4 cups) eggplant pared and
  cut into cubes
1-½ teaspoons salt
2 tablespoons flour
1 cup cheddar cheese, shredded
1/4 cup green pepper, chopped
1/4 cup onion, chopped
2 cups tomatoes, cooked or canned
2 cups lamb, cooked, diced
3/4 cup bread cubes, toasted

Combine eggplant, green pepper, onion, and salt. Add tomatoes, reserving 3 tablespoons juice. Simmer vegetables 10 minutes. Preheat oven to 350 degrees F. (moderate). Grease a 2-quart casserole. Mix flour with reserved tomato juice; stir into vegetables. Simmer until mixture thickens, about 3 minutes. Place half the lamb in casserole. Add half the vegetables and half the cheese. Repeat layers. Top with bread cubes. Bake 20 minutes, or until eggplant is tender.

POULTRY

TURKEY — THAT NOBLE BIRD!!!
CHICKEN — THE CONSTANT FAVORITE!!!

Both are among our most economical buys just now. Some special recipes to appeal to just about everyone are featured here. GET COOKING!!!

ROASTED TURKEY WITH ORANGE SAUCE

1. Thaw turkey in original bag (do not puncture or open) using one of the following three methods:
   A. Place turkey on tray in refrigerator...3-4 days.
   B. Place on tray at room temperature in a closed grocery bag (bag prevents skin from becoming too warm)...1 hour per pound.
   C. Cover with cold water, changing water frequently..½ hour per pound. Refrigerate or cook as soon as thawed.
2. Remove plastic bag...remove neck and giblets from cavities...rinse turkey and wipe dry.
3. No need to stuff turkey. If desired, insert slices of fresh orange in cavity of turkey for extra flavor.
4. Fasten down legs either by tying or tucking under skin band. Neck skin should be skewered to back and wings twisted akimbo.
5. To roast, place turkey breast up on rack in shallow roasting pan. Brush with melted butter. Insert roast-meat thermometer into thick part of thigh. Roast in pre-heated 325 degree F. oven. Time chart here given is guide to roasting time. If desired, a "tent" of foil may be placed loosely over turkey to keep from becoming too brown. About 30 minutes before turkey is scheduled to be done, baste with Orange/Butter Marinade (recipe follows) and continue doing so at frequent intervals. Turkey is done when roast-meat thermometer registers 180-185 degrees F. or when drumstick and thigh move easily and thick part of drumstick feels soft when pressed with thumb and forefinger.

TIME CHART FOR ROASTING STUFFED TURKEY IN PREHEATED 325 DEGREE OVEN*

Because turkeys vary from one to another due to conformation, variety, etc., cooking times can be only approximate. Because of this it would be well to allow an extra half hour of roasting time in case turkey needs that extra cooking. Check for doneness during last hour of roasting.

READY-TO-COOK WEIGHT	APPROXIMATE COOKING TIME
6 pounds	3 hours
8 pounds	3-½ hours
12 pounds	4-½ hours
16 pounds	5-½ hours
20 pounds	6-½ hours

Roast meat Thermometer, all at 180-185 degrees F.

*NOTE: Unstuffed turkeys require about ½ hour less roasting time.

ORANGE/BUTTER MARINADE

   1 cup butter
   1/4 cup honey
   1/3 cup frozen orange juice concentrate

Combine ingredients in small saucepan and simmer together for 5 minutes, stirring constantly. Use for basting turkey last 30 minutes of roasting. If desired, serve additional sauce with turkey.

BUTTER—BASTED TURKEY WITH SAUSAGE-CORN BREAD DRESSING

For one 16 to 18 lb. turkey and one 2 qt. casserole
2 cups chopped celery
1/4 cup chopped onion
1/4 cup (½ stick) butter
1 pan corn bread, coarsely crumbled*
8 cups dry bread cubes
1-½ lb. pork sausage meat cooked,
    crumbled and drained
1 teaspoon sage
½ teaspoon pepper
2 eggs, beaten
1-3/4 cups water
One 16 to 18 lb. turkey

Saute celery and onion in butter until tender. Combine corn bread, bread cubes, sausage, sage and pepper in very large bowl. Add celery and onion, mixing lightly. Gradually add eggs and water, tossing lightly. Lightly stuff about 2/3 of dressing into body cavity and neck region of turkey. Roast according to standard roasting directions. Baste frequently with melted butter. Bake remaining dressing in a covered 2-qt. casserole during last 45 minutes of roasting time.

*CORN BREAD

1½ cups enriched corn meal
1½ cups all-purpose flour
½ teaspoon salt
4 teaspoons baking powder
2 eggs
1-½ cups milk
1/4 cup (½ stick) butter, soft

Sift together dry ingredients into bowl. Add eggs, milk and butter. Beat with rotary beater until smooth, about 1 minute. Do not overbeat. Pour batter into buttered 9-inch square baking pan. Bake in preheated hot oven (425 degrees F.) about 25 minutes or until golden brown. (this amount is just right for the Sausage Corn Bread Dressing.)
NOTE: Prepare corn bread 1 or 2 days in advance; cover.

TURKEY-NOODLE BAKE

6 servings
4-ounce package noodles (about 2 cups uncooked)
2 chicken bouillon cubes
pepper, as desired
1 tablespoon chopped pimiento
2 cups cooked turkey, cubed
3/4 cup shredded sharp process cheese
1/4 cup flour
2 cups mushroom liquid and water
1/4 teaspoon salt
½ teaspoon poultry seasoning
4-ounce can mushroom stems and pieces,
    drained, chopped
1/3 cup fine dry breadcrumbs
1 tablespoon butter or margarine

Cook noodles as directed on package; drain. In a saucepan, blend flour with a little of the liquid to make a paste. Gradually stir in remaining liquid. Add bouillon cubes and seasonings. Bring to a boil, stirring constantly. Reduce heat to simmer; cook 1 minute longer, stirring as needed. Add pimiento and mushroom to sauce. In a 2-quart casserole place half the noodles and half the turkey in layers. Cover with half the sauce. Repeat layers. Top with cheese; sprinkle with breadcrumbs; dot with fat. Bake, uncovered, at 350 degrees F. 30 to 40 minutes or until bubbly and browned.

TURKEY-HAM CURRY

6 servings, ½ cup each
2 teaspoons onion, chopped
2 tablespoons butter or margarine
½ teaspoon salt
Few grains pepper
1 cup turkey, cooked, diced
6 slices toast
1 tablespoon green pepper, chopped
1/4 cup flour
1/4 teaspoon curry powder
2-1/4 cups milk
½ cup ham, cooked, diced

Brown the onion and green pepper lightly in the fat. Stir in the flour and seasonings. Add milk slowly, stirring constantly. Cook until thickened. Add turkey and ham. Heat to serving temperature. Serve on toast.
NOTE: you may serve turkey-ham curry on cooked rice instead of toast if you prefer.

CHICKEN AND FRUIT PAELLA

1/4 cup all-purpose flour
1 teaspoon salt
Dash of pepper
2-½ to 3 pound broiler-fryer, cut-up
3 tablespoons butter
1 medium onion, sliced (about 1 cup)
1 cup sliced fresh mushrooms
1 package (6 ounce) long grain and wild rice
2 teaspoons chicken seasoned stock base*

1/4 teaspoon whole saffron OR 1/8 teaspoon
  ground saffron
1-½ cups milk
1 cup water
1 can (13-½ ounces) pineapple chunks, drained
1 can (11 ounces) mandarin oranges, drained
1 medium green pepper, cut into ½ inch
  wide strips
1 medium tomato cut into wedges

Combine flour, salt and pepper in plastic or paper bag. Add chicken pieces one at a time and shake to coat evenly. In a large fry pan, melt butter; slowly brown chicken. Remove chicken. Add onion and mushrooms; saute' until tender. Combine rice, including seasonings, chicken stock base and saffron. Remove fry pan from heat. Stir rice mixture, milk and water into fry pan. Add chicken. Bring to a boil; cover tightly and simmer 25 minutes or until chicken is tender. Gently stir in pineapple, oranges, green pepper and tomato. Cover and heat through. Makes 4-6 servings.
Note: 1 chicken bouillon cube may be used in place of 2 teaspoons chicken seasoned stock base.

HUNGARIAN BAKED CHICKEN AND CABBAGE

(Pictured, page 42)

1 three pound chicken, disjointed
3 tablespoons butter
Salt
Pepper
1 head green cabbage, (about 2 Lb.)
1 onion, sliced into thin rings
2 red apples, cored and sliced
1 tablespoon grated lemon peel
2 teaspoons caraway seed
1 teaspoon sugar
2 cups (8 ounces) shredded Swiss cheese
4 tablespoons slivered almonds
Paprika
1 tablespoon chopped fresh parsley

Melt 3 tablespoons butter in 13x9x2 inch baking pan. Dip chicken in butter and turn skin side up in pan. Sprinkle with salt and pepper. Bake in preheated 400 degree F. oven about 1 hour. Meanwhile, slice cabbage into ½ inch thick slices. Place in 3-quart buttered baking dish. Cover with onion rings, then apple slices. Sprinkle lemon peel, caraway seed and sugar over all. Cover tightly with foil and place in oven along with chicken after chicken has baked 25 minutes. Bake both about 35 minutes, or until chicken is tender and cabbage is cooked, but still crisp. To serve: Sprinkle 1 cup cheese over cabbage. Place chicken servings on each cabbage slice. Pour over chicken drippings from pan. Sprinkle 1 cup cheese and almonds over chicken. Sprinkle with paprika. Place under broiler until cheese melts. Garnish with parsley. Makes 6 servings.

CHICKEN PARMESAN

1 egg
2 pounds chicken parts
½ cup Italian-flavored bread crumbs
2 tablespoons shortening
1 can (10-3/4 ounces) Campbell's Tomato Soup
1/4 cup water
1/4 cup chopped onion
½ teaspoon each garlic powder, basil and
    oregano leaves, crushed
Shredded Mozzarella cheese

Beat egg and 1 tablespoon water. Roll chicken in egg mixture, then crumbs. In skillet, brown chicken in shortening; pour off fat. Stir in soup, 1/4 cup water, onion, and seasonings. Cover; cook over low heat 45 minutes or until done. Stir occasionally. Sprinkle with cheese; heat until cheese melts. Serve with grated Parmesan cheese and additional oregano leaves if desired. Makes 4 servings.

FARMER'S CHICKEN STEW

1 5-lb. stewing chicken, cut-up
2 cups water
3 small onions, cut in half
5 whole cloves
1 bay leaf
1 tablespoon salt
1-½ teaspoons paprika
1/4 teaspoon pepper
2 cups carrot slices, cut diagonally in ½-inch pieces
2 cups celery slices, cut diagonally in ½-inch pieces
1-10-ounce package frozen peas, unthawed
2 cups milk
½ cup flour

Place chicken in 4-quart Dutch oven. Add water, onions and seasonings. Bring to a boil. Cover, simmer 2½ to 3 hours or until chicken is tender. Remove bay leaf and cloves. Add vegetables; bring to a boil. Cover; simmer 15 to 20 minutes or until vegetables are tender. Drain and reserve broth. Skim off excess fat. Pour 3 cups broth into sauce pan. (If necessary, add water to measure 3 cups). Gradually add milk to flour, stirring until smooth. Add to hot broth; bring to a boil over medium heat, stirring constantly until gravy is thickened. Pour gravy over chicken and vegetables. Heat thoroughly. Sprinkle with paprika before serving if desired. 6 servings.

CHICKEN A LA KING

6 servings
1 cup frozen green peas
1/4 cup chopped green pepper
2/3 cup flour
2 cups chicken broth
pepper, as desired
2 cups diced cooked chicken or turkey
1 tablespoon chopped pimiento
2 tablespoons finely chopped onion
1/3 cup boiling water
1 cup cold milk
2 teaspoons salt
½ teaspoon poultry seasoning
1 can (4 ounces) mushroom stems and pieces,
    drained and chopped
Cooked rice, toast, or biscuits

Cook peas, onion, and green pepper in boiling water in a covered pan 5 minutes, Drain; save the liquid. Blend flour with milk. Combine vegetable cooking liquid, broth, and seasonings; slowly stir in flour mixture. Bring to a boil, stirring constantly, cook 1 minute. Add chicken, cooked vegetables, mushrooms, and pimiento. Heat thoroughly and serve on rice, toast, or biscuits.

CREAMED CHICKEN OR TURKEY

6 servings, 2/3 cup each
1-½ cups chicken or turkey broth
½ teaspoon salt
½ teaspoon poultry seasoning
6 slices toast
Parsley-few sprigs
1/3 cup flour
1-½ cups milk
1/8 teaspoon pepper
2 cups chicken or turkey, cooked, diced
1/4 cup butter or margarine

Melt fat; blend in flour. Stir in liquids, seasonings, and chicken or turkey. Cook and stir until thickened. Serve on toast. Garnish with parsley.

TURKEY AND DUMPLINGS

6 servings, 3 ounces meat and 2 dumplings each
½ cup flour
4 cups hot turkey broth or chicken bouillon
1 cup flour
½ cup milk
1/3 cup water
1 quart cooked turkey, large pieces
Salt (as needed)
1-½ teaspoons baking powder
½ teaspoon salt

Mix ½ cup flour with the water to make a smooth paste. Gradually blend into the hot broth or bouillon. Cook, stirring constantly, until thickened. Add turkey and salt as needed. Simmer, covered, while preparing dumplings. Stir occasionally. Mix 1 cup flour, baking powder, and ½ teaspoon salt thoroughly. Add milk, stirring 18 times. Drop dough from a tablespoon onto the meat and broth, making 12 dumplings. Cover tightly and simmer fifteen minutes without lifting the cover of the pan.

TURKEY-MUSHROOM SCALLOP

6 servings, 3-½ by 2-½ inches each
1-½ cups mushrooms, chopped
1 tablespoon flour
1 cup milk
1 tablespoon parsley, chopped
2 eggs, beaten
1/8 teaspoon pepper
1 can mushroom sauce
1/4 cup butter or margarine
1 cup breadcrumbs, soft
1 cup turkey, cooked, coarsely chopped
1/4 teaspoon salt
1/8 teaspoon onion juice

Preheat oven to 375 degrees F. (moderate). Grease a 7x7x3 inch baking dish. Brown mushrooms lightly in the fat. Stir flour into mushroom mixture. Add breadcrumbs. Add milk slowly, stirring constantly. Cook over low heat 5 minutes. Add turkey, parsley, eggs, and seasonings to mushroom mixture. Pour into baking dish. Set in a pan of hot water. Bake 40 minutes, or until firm. Cut into rectangles. Serve hot mushroom sauce over each serving.

HOMEMADE NOODLES WITH CHICKEN

6 servings
1 cup flour
1 tablespoon half-and-half or table cream
3/4 teaspoon poultry seasoning
5 cups chicken broth
paprika
1 egg or 1/4 cup egg yolks (3 or 4 yolks), slightly beaten
1-½ teaspoon salt
pepper, as desired
3 cups cubed cooked chicken
parsley

Combine flour, egg yolks and cream thoroughly and form into a ball. Do not knead. Divide into two parts. Roll each part on lightly floured surface until paper thin. Allow dough to dry 5 to 10 minutes. With a thin sharp knife, cut dough into strips of desired width and length. Add seasonings to broth; bring to a boil. Add noodles and boil 9 to 12 minutes, or until tender. Add chicken and continue cooking only until chicken is hot. Sprinkle with paprika and garnish with parsley.

CORNISH GAME HENS WITH CHEESY RICE STUFFING

1/4 cup (½ stick) butter
1/3 cup regular rice
2 tablespoons diced celery
2 tablespoons finely chopped onion
1 cup chicken broth
1 can (2 ounces) mushrooms, drained and chopped
1 cup (4 ounces) shredded Cheddar cheese
2 1-pound Cornish Game Hens
salt
pepper
melted butter

In a 1-½-quart saucepan melt butter; add rice, celery and onion. Cook 5-10 minutes, stirring frequently. Add chicken broth and bring mixture to a boil. Cover and simmer over low heat about 20 minutes or until liquid is absorbed and rice is fluffy. Stir in mushrooms. Cool. Toss cheese lightly with cooled rice mixture. Meanwhile season birds inside with salt and pepper. Stuff birds with rice mixture. Place on rack, breast side up in shallow baking pan. Baste with butter. Loosely cover with foil. Roast in preheated 400 degree F. oven for 30 minutes. Remove foil; continue roasting for 45 minutes uncovered or until done. Occasionally baste with butter during last 45 minutes of roasting.
Note: Any additional stuffing may be placed in small baking dish, covered and baked during last 45 minutes of roasting time. Remove cover for last 15 minutes.

COUNTRY CHICKEN COOKED IN MILK

1-3½ pound frying chicken, cut up
1/4 cup flour
½ teaspoon dry mustard
½ teaspoon paprika
1-½ teaspoon salt
1/4 cup melted butter
1-½ cups milk
1/8 teaspoon pepper

Wash chicken and pat dry. Mix flour and seasonings. Roll chicken in mixture and shake off excess flour. Melt butter in large fry pan. Fry chicken slowly until golden on all sides. Transfer chicken to shallow baking pan or dish. Add milk to fry pan. Heat and stir until all brown bits are loosened into milk mixture. Pour over chicken. Bake uncovered in moderate oven, 350 degrees F. until tender, about 45 minutes.

CHICKEN POLYNESIAN

6 servings
6 chicken half-breasts
2 teaspoons salt
1/4 cup flour
1/4 cup water
1/4 teaspoon ginger
1-½ teaspoons curry powder
1 cup buttermilk, cultured
1 clove garlic, cut in pieces
3 tablespoons fat or oil
1/4 cup onion, chopped
1 whole clove
2 tablespoons almonds, chopped or slivered, toasted

Marinate chicken in buttermilk, combined with salt and garlic for 1 hour. Drain chicken, save liquid. Roll chicken pieces in flour. Brown in fat or oil about 10 minutes. Add water, cover, and cook slowly until chicken is tender — about 1 hour. Remove chicken from pan and keep warm. Cook onion in pan drippings until tender. Skim off excess fat. Remove garlic from buttermilk. Mix spices with buttermilk. Add to onion. Heat, stirring constantly, until thickened. Remove clove. Serve chicken topped with sauce and garnished with almonds.

CREAMED EGGS ON TOAST

6 servings, about 3/4 cup each
1/4 cup margarine
2 teaspoons Worcestershire sauce
1 teaspoon salt
8 hard-cooked eggs, sliced
1/4 cup flour
2 teaspoons prepared mustard
3 cups milk
6 slices toast

Melt fat; blend in flour. Add seasonings. Gradually stir in milk. Cook constantly, until thickened. Add eggs; do not stir. Heat to serving temperature. Serve on toast.

CHICKEN CURRY

6 servings, 1 cup each
10-½ ounce can cream of chicken soup, condensed
3 cups chicken, cooked, diced
½ cup olives, stuffed, sliced
2 cups (about 2/3 cup uncooked) rice, cooked
2/3 cup evaporated milk
3/4 teaspoon curry powder
1 cup pineapple chunks, canned, drained
parsley, if desired

Combine soup, milk, and curry powder. Heat slowly, stirring until well blended. Add chicken, pineapple chunks, and olives. Heat to serving temperature. Serve over rice. Garnish with parsley, if desired.

CHICKEN PAPRIKA

6 servings
3 chicken thighs
1-½ teaspoon salt
1/4 cup flour
1/4 cup onions, diced
2 teaspoons lemon juice
2 cups sour cream
2 cups (about 4 ounces uncooked) cooked noodles
3 chicken half-breasts
1/8 teaspoon pepper
2 tablespoons fat or oil
1 cup hot water
3 tablespoons flour
2 teaspoons paprika

Season chicken with salt and pepper. Roll chicken in 1/4 cup flour. Brown chicken slowly in hot fat or oil, 10 to 15 minutes. Add onions, hot water, and lemon juice. Cook, covered, over low heat about 40 minutes or until chicken is tender. Remove chicken from pan and keep warm. Blend 3 tablespoons flour with ½ cup of sour cream. Stir into drippings in the pan. Add remaining sour cream. Simmer, uncovered 5 minutes. Add paprika and mix well. Place chicken on cooked noodles, and pour sour cream sauce over top.

CHICKEN DIVAN

3 chicken breasts, cooked, boned and sliced
2 packages (10-ounces each) frozen OR 2 pounds
     fresh broccoli, cooked and well drained
½ cup grated Parmesan cheese
2 cups Mousseline Sause

Arrange broccoli in bottom of shallow gratin pan or 2-quart casserole. Sprinkle with 1/4 cup Parmesan cheese. Arrange sliced chicken over broccoli. Pour on Mousseline Sauce. Sprinkle with remaining Parmesan cheese. Broil about 5 inches from heat 3 to 5 minutes or until Parmesan cheese is lightly browned. Serve at once. This sauce does not stand well or reheat. 4 to 6 servings.
TIPS: Prepare Hollandaise first; let cool before adding whipped cream. If chicken and broccoli are cooked ahead, place in 350 degree F. oven, covered with foil, to heat for 15 minutes before adding Mousseline sauce. Broil as directed.

MOUSSELINE SAUCE
(WHIPPED CREAM WITH HOLLANDAISE)
Yield: 2 cups

Hollandaise Sauce:
     ½ cup (1 stick) butter
     4 egg yolks
     2 tablespoons lemon juice
     1/4 cup boiling water
     1/4 teaspoons salt

     ½ cup whipping cream

Beat butter at high speed of mixer until light and fluffy. Add egg yolks, one at a time, beating well after each addition. Continue beating at high speed and very gradually add lemon juice, water and salt. (Mixture will thin out). Transfer to a heavy saucepan and cook over low heat, stirring constantly, until thickened. Cool to room temperature. Whip cream until very stuff, fold into cooled Hollandaise Sauce. Use for Chicken Divan, asparagus, broccoli, artichokes, eggs or poached fish.

CHICKEN SAUCE

1-½ cups sauce
1 tablespoon butter or other fat
1/4 teaspoon salt
3 tablespoons flour
1-½ cups chicken broth

Melt fat over low heat; blend in flour and salt. Heat and stir until bubbly. Add broth slowly, stirring constantly. Cook over low heat, stirring constantly, until thickened.
Chicken Bouillon sauce — In place of chicken broth, use a mixture of 1-½ cups milk and three chicken-flavored bouillon cubes.

CHICKEN CROQUETTS

6 servings, 2 croquettes each
2 cups chicken, cooked, diced
½ cup celery, finely chopped
2 tablespoons onion, finely chopped
1/4 teaspoon poultry seasoning
1/4 cup evaporated milk
2 quarts oil for frying
1/3 cup nuts, chopped
1 cup (about 1/3 cup, uncooked) rice, cooked
1 teaspoon flour
1 egg, beaten
3/4 cup breadcrumbs, fine, dry
chicken sauce, 1 recipe
1/8 teaspoon salt

Combine chicken, rice, vegetables, flour and seasonings. Add egg and enough milk to moisten. Shape into 12 croquettes. Roll in breadcrumbs. Heat oil in a deep kettle or deep-fat fryer to 375 degrees F. Fry croquettes until browned, 2 to 5 minutes. Drain on paper. Serve hot chicken sauce over croquettes. Garnish with nuts.

HERB-CHICKEN PIECES

6 servings
3 chicken half-breasts
1 cup sour cream
1/8 teaspoon pepper
10-½ ounce can cream of mushroom soup, condensed
3 chicken thighs
1 teaspoon salt
1 cup packaged herb-seasoned bread stuffing mix,
     crushed
½ cup milk

Marinate chicken pieces in sour cream in refrigerator overnight. Preheat oven to 350 degrees F. (moderate). Grease a shallow baking pan. Drain off sour cream; reserve for sauce. Season chicken with salt and pepper. Roll in stuffing mix. Place in baking pan, skin side down. Bake 30 minutes. Turn and bake 30 minutes longer, or until tender. Thin the soup with the milk. Combine soup mixture with reserved sour cream; heat well. Serve sauce and chicken separately.

SCRAMBLED EGGS, DEVILED

6 eggs
One 2¼ ounce can deviled ham
Dash pepper
2 tablespoons water
2 tablespoons butter or margarine

Prepare as for regular scrambled eggs. Mix in deviled ham quite throughly. Melt butter or margarine in fry pan. Pour in mixture and cook slowly 5 to 7 minutes to desired doneness. Serves 4.

CHEESE DISHES

Interestingly, the special touch of cheese dates to its discovery about 4,000 years ago. Legend has it that a shepherd boy carried milk in a pouch. Rennet from the lining of that pouch, combined with heat from the sun, caused a separation of the milk into curds (solids) and whey (liquid). The shepherd boy found the curds delicious.

Today we can buy about 200 varieties of domestic cheese. Some are called simply, "American," by which most people mean a process cheese made from Cheddar in combination with other ingredients. Cheddar, named after an English town, is the most popular selling cheese in America, accounting for a large percent of the market. Others have far-away, foreign-sounding names like Gorgonzola, Camembert, Port du Salut or Brie, but these and many others are American-made.

One of the best qualities about cheese is that it's an instant, no-waste food, an important consideration in these economy-conscious times. That means it can be eaten right after purchasing by cutting or slicing without the loss of a crumb.

Some cheeses are dessert cheeses. They're meant to be eaten as is. Notable examples are Camembert or Brie, Port du Salut or Limburger. Match with fruits or serve "au naturel." Cheeses can add charm and substance to salads whether it's in strips or cubes for the main dish or Julienne salad or one with fruits. Blue cheese or the Italian variety, Gorgonzola, are famous for crumbly quality in green salads. And we should not forget the Feta cheese the Greek people use in their green salads. Delicious!!!

Whatever the variety, cheese is a first-class protein food. Ounce for ounce, cheese matches the protein quality of meat, fish or fowl. It can add the special touch to your own menus, lifting them from humdrum to high level.

CLASSIC QUICHE LORRAINE

6 servings

Crust:
- 1 cup all-purpose flour
- 1/4 teaspoon salt
- 3 tablespoons butter
- 2 tablespoons lard
- 3 to 4 tablespoons cold water

Filling:
- 2 cups (8 ounces) shredded Swiss cheese
- 6 slices bacon, cooked, drained, crumbled
- ½ cup chopped green onion with tops
- 2 cups light cream OR half and half
- 1 tablespoon cornstarch
- 4 eggs, slightly beaten
- ½ teaspoon salt
- 1/4 teaspoon nutmeg
- dash cayenne pepper
- 2 tablespoons grated Parmesan cheese

Heat oven to 375 degrees F. For crust, combine flour and salt. Cut in butter and lard until mixture resembles coarse crumbs. Gradually add water, 1 tablespoon at a time, mixing just until dough holds together. Shape into a ball. Roll out on a lightly floured surface to a 13-inch circle. Line a 9-inch pie plate with dough. Trim and build up edges with a high flute. (continued, top of next column)

For filling, toss together cheese, bacon and green onion; place in pie crust. Stir a small amount of cream into the cornstarch until smooth. Add remaining cream, eggs, salt, nutmeg and cayenne. Pour over cheese mixture. Sprinkle with Parmesan cheese. Bake in preheated oven about 40 minutes. Let stand 10 minutes before serving. Garnish with fresh tomato wedges and parsley, if desired.

CHEESE FONDUE

- 4 cups (1 lb.) shredded Cheddar cheese
- 1½ cups (6 ounces) shredded Provolone cheese
- 1/4 cup all-purpose flour
- 2-1/4 cups apple juice or cider
- ½ teaspoon nutmeg

Mix cheeses with flour. Heat apple juice to boiling in saucepan. Stir in cheese a little at a time. Continue heating, stirring until cheese melts and forms a smooth mixture. Add nutmeg. Transfer to fondue pot. Serve with apple, pear and melon chunks for dipping. Yield: approx. 4 cups.

CHEESE OMELET WITH CURRANT JELLY

4 egg yolks
Dash of white pepper
4 egg whites
1/4 cup water
1/4 teaspoon salt

1/4 teaspoon cream of tartar
2 teaspoons butter
½ cup currant jelly
3/4 cup (3 ounces) shredded Cheddar cheese
1 tablespoon butter, softened

Beat egg yolks and pepper until thick and lemon-colored. Beat egg whites, water, salt and cream of tarter until stiff but not dry. Fold yolks into whites. Melt butter in 10-inch omelet pan or a 10-inch skillet with heatproof handle. Heat until just hot enough to sizzle a drop of water. Turn mixture into skillet. Cook over low heat on top of range until puffy and browned on bottom (about 5 minutes). Transfer to preheated 325 degree oven and bake 10-12 minutes or until knife inserted near center comes out clean. Meanwhile break up jelly with fork; mix ½ cup (2 ounces) cheese with butter. Remove omelet from oven and change oven to broil. Turn omelet onto heatproof platter. Score down the center with a spatula. Place jelly on bottom. Fold omelet in half and top with cheese-butter mixture. Sprinkle on remaining cheese. Broil until cheese melts. Serve immediately. 2-3 servings.

GOURMET PIZZA

CRUST:
2-2/3 cups all-purpose flour
1/3 cup grated Parmesan cheese
2-½ teaspoons baking powder
1 teaspoon salt
1/4 cup (½ stick) butter
1/4 cup lard
3/4 cup milk

FILLING:
2 pounds mild Italian sausage
1 can (8 ounces) tomato sauce
1 teaspoon oregano
1 teaspoon sweet basil, crumbled
1 clove garlic, minced
4 medium tomatoes, thinly sliced
Green pepper strips
½ pound small fresh mushrooms, thickly sliced
4 cups (1 pound) grated Mozzarella cheese
2 tablespoons grated Parmesan cheese

To prepare Crust: Combine flour, 1/3 cup Parmesan cheese, baking powder and salt. Cut in butter and lard until mixture resembles coarse meal. Gradually add milk; mix at low speed on electric mixer until mixture leaves sides of bowl. Gather dough together and press into ball. Knead dough in bowl 10 times or until smooth. Divide in half. On lightly floured surface, roll each half into 13-inch circle. Transfer to two 12-inch pizza pans, buttered and dusted with Parmesan cheese; crimp edges. Partially bake in preheated 425 degree oven, 9 minutes. Remove to wire rack to cool.

To prepare filling: Break sausage in bits into skillet and lightly brown, stirring occasionally. Divide cooked sausage into two portions. Mix together tomato sauce, oregano, basil and garlic. Assemble each pizza as follows: Evenly distribute one-half of the sauce over the bottom, one-half of the sausage; sprinkle over 1 cup Mozzarella cheese. Arrange a layer of tomato slices, pepper strips and mushroom slices on top, over all sprinkle 1 cup Mozzarella cheese and 1 table-spoon Parmesan cheese. Bake in preheated 425 degree oven, 20-25 minutes. Yield: 2 pizzas.

MORNING MUFFIN

2 English muffins, split
4 slices Canadian-style bacon, 1/4 inch thick
4 slices pineapple
4 slices (1 ounce each) Swiss cheese

Place muffins and bacon on broiler pan; broil. Remove muffins when toasted, butter; keep warm. Turn bacon; add pineapple slices and broil until bacon is done and pineapple warm. Place bacon on muffin. Top with pineapple slice. Cut cheese in half. Place two halves over each sandwich. Broil until cheese melts. Garnish with paprika and parsley. Makes 4 servings.

CHEESE CREPES WITH SAUCE ROYALE

Yield: 4 servings
Baking dish, 1-½-quart
Preheated 350 degree F. oven
8 cooked crepes*
1-½ cups cottage cheese
nutmeg

SAUCE
2 tablespoons sugar
1 teaspoon cornstarch
½ cup orange juice
1 teaspoon butter
1 cup fresh strawberries

Place 3 tablespoons cottage cheese on each crepe; sprinkle with nutmeg. Roll; place in baking dish. Bake 15-20 minutes or until heated through. Meanwhile prepare sauce. In a 1-quart saucepan combine sugar and cornstarch; stir in orange juice. Cook over medium heat, stirring constantly, until thickened; boil 2 additional minutes. Stir in butter. Remove from heat. Stir in strawberries. Serve 2 crepes per serving with 1/4 cup strawberry sauce. 290 calories per serving.

Note: Sauce may be made ahead to the point of adding strawberries. Reheat when ready to serve and add strawberries.

*CREPES

Yield:16
Skillet, 8-inch
3 tablespoons butter
3/4 cup all-purpose flour
1/4 teaspoon salt
3 eggs
1 cup milk

In skillet melt butter. Combine flour and salt. Add eggs, milk and melted butter (set aside skillet), beat with a rotary beater until smooth. Heat buttered skillet over medium-low heat. For each crepe pour a scant 2 tablespoons batter in skillet; immediately rotate pan. Cook until light brown; turn and brown other side. Stack between sheets of waxed paper or paper toweling until ready to use.

Note: Crepes may be made ahead, wrapped and refrigerated for overnight or frozen for longer storage. Remove from freezer as needed.

CHEESE-STUFFED MUSHROOMS

20 fresh mushrooms, 1-½ inches in diameter
Fresh lemon juice
Salt
1 cup (4 ounces) shredded Cheddar cheese
1/4 cup crushed herb seasoned croutons
Bacon, cooked

Pull stems from washed mushrooms. Dip mushroom caps in lemon juice. Lightly sprinkle cavity with salt. Mix cheese and croutons; spoon into mushroms. Top each filled mushroom with a small square of bacon. Place on baking sheet; bake in pre-heated 400 degree F. oven, 10-12 minutes. Yield 20.

FARMER'S CHOP SUEY

1 pound carton cottage cheese
1 pound carton dairy sour cream
1 teaspoon salt
1 cup unpeeled sliced cucumbers
2 cups torn lettuce
3 green onions with tops, chopped
½ cup sliced radishes
½ cup sliced green pepper
½ cup celery thinly sliced on diagonal
2 hard-cooked eggs, quartered
Cherry tomatoes, halved

Mix cottage cheese, sour cream and salt. Chill for 1 hour. Cut cucumber slices in half, if large; salt and chill. Drain before adding to salad. Place lettuce in large salad bowl; spoon over cottage cheese mixture. Arrange cucumbers, onions, radishes, green pepper, celery, eggs and tomatoes on top. Toss all together and serve. Yield 7 cups.

CHEESE RAREBIT

6 servings, ½ cup each
3 cups (12 ounces) process cheddar cheese, shredded
1 teaspoon Worcestershire sauce
2 tablespoons pimiento, chopped
1-1/4 cups milk
1 egg, beaten
½ teaspoon dry mustard
6 or 12 slices toast

Combine all ingredients except pimiento and toast. Cook over low heat, stirring constantly, until cheese melts and mixture is slightly thickened. Stir in pimiento and serve immediately on toast.

SPANISH RICE WITH CHEESE

6 servings
3 slices bacon
1/4 cup chopped green pepper
1 cup water
3/4 cup packaged precooked rice
1 teaspoon sugar
1 cup shredded Cheddar cheese
1 small onion, finely chopped
1/4 cup chopped celery
½ teaspoon salt
2 cups cooked or canned tomatoes
1/4 teaspoons Worcestershire sauce

Fry bacon in a heavy 2-quart saucepan. Drain bacon on paper. In 1 tablespoon bacon drippings, lightly brown onion, green pepper, and celery. Add water and salt; bring to a boil. Stir in rice, tomatoes, sugar, and Worcestershire sauce. Simmer until rice is just tender, stirring occasionally. Crumble bacon and stir into rice mixture. Sprinkle cheese over top. Cover and continue cooking over very low heat until cheese is melted, about 5 minutes.

POTATO CHEESE PUFF

6 servings, about 1 cup each
3 beaten egg yolks
3 cups mashed potatoes, seasoned
1 tablespoon parsley, chopped
3 egg whites, stiffly beaten
1/4 cup milk
1 teaspoon onion, grated
2 cups cheese or process cheese food, coarsely shredded
Preheat oven to 375 degrees F.

Grease a 2-quart baking dish. Combine egg yolks and milk. Add remaining ingredients except egg whites; beat well. Fold egg whites into mixture. Put in baking dish. Bake 40 to 45 minutes or until a knife inserted in the center comes out clean and the top is browned. Serve immediately.

VEGETABLES, SALADS AND DRESSINGS

In the last several years with our changing life styles, some of us have not given enough thought to the many varieties of vegetables available to us. The pattern of eating at fast-food operations has grown and many restaurant menus have minimized the vegetable aspect in our diet.

This section is devoted to some interesting and easy vegetable combinations. So good for us, nutrition-wise, we should get back into the vegetable habit again. It's not hard!!! And we will have healthier families for it!!! Try a new vegetable recipe today!!! Experience a new taste treat!!!

HUNGARIAN CABBAGE

6 servings
2 slices bacon
3/4 teaspoon salt
2 tablespoons vinegar
2 quarts coarsely shredded cabbage
Pepper, as desired
2 tablespoons water

Fry bacon until crisp; remove from pan. Add remaining ingredients to fat in pan. Cover tightly and cook over low heat, stirring occasionally, for 20 to 25 minutes. Cabbage should be tender but crisp. Crumble bacon over top before serving.

BAKED CARROTS AND CELERY

4 cups raw carrots, cut in strips
3 tablespoons butter or margarine
½ teaspoon salt
Dash pepper
1 cup celery, diced
1/3 cup water

Put carrots in casserole. Mix with other ingredients. Cover. Bake until tender, 350 degrees F. 25-30 minutes. Remove cover for escape of excess moisture. Serves 6.

DILLY CARROTS AND BEANS

6 servings (½ cup each)
3/4 cup water
½ teaspoon salt
½ pound green snap beans
1/4 cup Italian dressing
1 teaspoon sugar
½ teaspoon dill seed
4 carrots, medium size

Combine water, sugar, salt, and dill seed in a saucepan; bring to boiling. Wash and trim green beans; leave whole. Add to boiling water. Simmer 5 minutes. Cut carrots into thin strips, 2 to 3 inches long. Add to green beans. Boil until both vegetables are tender and liquid is almost evaporated — about 10 minutes. Add Italian dressing and toss to mix well. Serve hot, or chill and use in tossed vegetable salads.

CHINESE-STYLE CAULIFLOWER

6 servings (1/3 cup each)
1 head cauliflower florets, thinly sliced
2 tablespoons butter or margarine
chives or parsley, cut-up as desired
1 teaspoon salt
1/3 cup water, hot
2 tablespoons cream

Place cauliflower in heavy pan, sprinkle with salt, and add hot water. Cook covered about 5 minutes or until slightly crisp. Add fat and cream. Heat for 1 or 2 minutes longer. Garnish with cut-up chives or parsley.

QUICK CAULIFLOWER AU GRATIN

6 servings
2 packages (10 ounces each) frozen cauliflower
2 tablespoons fine dry breadcrumbs
1 can (10-½ ounces) condensed Cheddar
    cheese soup
1 teaspoon melted butter or margarine

Cook frozen cauliflower according to package directions. Drain cauliflower and place in a greased 1-quart casserole. Pour undiluted soup over cauliflower. Mix crumbs with fat and sprinkle over top. Bake at 350 degrees F. 20 to 30 minutes, or until sauce bubbles and crumbs are brown.

VEGETABLE MEDLEY

6 servings (½ cup each)
2 cups turnips, diced
½ cup water
1 cup green peas, fresh
½ teaspoon salt
1 cup carrots, sliced or diced
½ teaspoon salt
2 tablespoons butter or margarine
1/8 teaspoon pepper

Cook turnips and carrots for 10 minutes in boiling water with ½ teaspoon salt added. Add peas and cook until they are tender, about 5 to 7 minutes. Drain. Season with butter or margarine, salt, and pepper.

MEXICAN PANNED CORN

6 servings (½ cup each)
3 slices bacon
1/4 cup onion, chopped
1/4 cup green pepper, finely chopped
1 teaspoon salt
1 tablespoon bacon drippings
2 cans (12 ounces each) corn, drained vacuum packed
1/4 cup olives, stuffed green, chopped

Fry bacon until crisp. Drain on paper. Cook onion in bacon drippings just until tender. Add corn, green pepper, olives, and salt. Heat through stirring constantly. Crumble bacon over corn.

CORN FRITTERS

1 can corn, creamed
1-1/4 cup flour
1 teaspoon baking powder
½ teaspoon salt
2 eggs, separated

Add dry ingredients, mixed and sifted, to the corn. Then add egg yolks, beaten until thick, and fold in whites of eggs, beaten until stiff. Pan fry in fresh hot lard or other shortening, if you prefer. Drain on paper. Serve with maple syrup. Serves 4.

EGGPLANT-TOMATO CASSEROLE

6 servings, (3/4 cup each)
1 large onion, chopped
1/4 cup butter or margarine
1 teaspoon salt
1/4 cup corn flake crumbs
2 small eggplants, peeled and diced
28-ounce can tomatoes, drained
1/8 teaspoon pepper

Cook onion and eggplant in fat until golden brown. Add tomatoes, salt, and pepper. Mix thoroughly. Pour into casserole and top with the crumbs. Bake 30 minutes in 350 degree F. (moderate) oven.

GREEN BEAN-MUSHROOM CASSEROLE

6 servings
2 packages (10 ounces each) frozen cut green beans
1 teaspoon salt
1 can (4 ounces) mushroom stems and pieces, drained, chopped
1/4 cup finely chopped onion
1/4 cup water
1 can (10-½ ounces) condensed cream of mushroom soup
½ cup canned french-fried onion rings

Cook beans and chopped onion in water with salt until beans are tender, 12 to 15 minutes. Drain. Stir in undiluted soup and mushrooms. Pour into greased 1-½ quart casserole. Top with onion rings. Cover and bake at 350 degrees F. 30 minutes, or until mixture is heated through and top is brown.

LIMA BEAN CREOLE

6 servings
2 packages (10 ounces each) frozen lima beans
2 tablespoons chopped green pepper
2 cups cooked or canned tomatoes
6 slices bacon
1/4 cup finely chopped onion
½ teaspoon salt
pepper as desired

Cook beans as directed on package; drain. Fry bacon; drain on absorbent paper. In 2 tablespoons bacon drippings, brown onion and green pepper. Crumble bacon. Add browned onion and green pepper, bacon, seasonings, and tomatoes to beans. Cover and simmer gently 15 minutes.

ONIONS IN MUSHROOM SAUCE

6 servings
1-½ pounds small yellow onions
1 teaspoon salt
parsley
1 cup water
1 can (10-½ ounces) condensed cream of mushroom soup

Peel and quarter onions. Leave very small onions whole. Simmer onions in salted water 15 to 20 minutes, or until just tender. Drain. Add undiluted soup and simmer 10 to 15 minutes longer. Garnish with parsley before serving.

Did you know that the humble potato is native to Peru? And that when it was first introduced in Europe around 1500, people were apprehensive about eating it? They suspected the poor potato because it was a member of the Night-shade family of plants including tomatoes and bell peppers, supposedly noted for poisonous and narcotic properties.

It was the Irish peasants in Northern Europe who finally welcomed it as a good inexpensive food. In fact, the Irish may have been among the first people to truly appreciate the nutritional value of the potato. A medium-sized potato is an excellent source of Vitamin C and furnishes several B vitamins including thiamin, niacin and hard-to-get Vitamin B^6, such essential trace minerals as copper and magnesium and small amounts of iron and vegetable protein. At only 110 to 115 calories, the potato offers good nutritional return to us.

The classic Irish potato is simply boiled or steamed, usually whole in the skin to preserve all the good nutrition. But plain boiled potatoes are really just the beginning of many wonderful dishes. The chefs of Europe are masters at dressing up the humble boiled potato, and each country has its own special way of doing it. We have selected five special potato recipes from France, Switzerland, Germany and the Scandinavian countries. Hope you enjoy all of them!!!

CUSTARD POTATO CASSEROLE

(Pictured page 55)

(Universally Europe)
Blends well with all meats but especially tasty with ham.

6 medium potatoes (about 2 pounds)
   steamed or boiled
2 eggs, lightly beaten
½ teaspoon salt
Paprika

1-½ cups milk
½ tablespoon cornstarch
½ cup grated Parmesan cheese
Dash each pepper and nutmeg

Cut cooked potatoes into ½ inch slices. Arrange in shallow 2-quart casserole, set in pan of hot water. Mix milk and cornstarch in saucepan. Bring to boil, stirring. Remove from heat. Stir a little hot milk into eggs. Gradually pour into saucepan, stirring constantly. Stir in cheese, salt, pepper and nutmeg. Pour over potatoes. Bake in preheated 350 degree F. oven 20 to 25 minutes, or until custard is set. Sprinkle with paprika. 6 to 8 servings.

FONDUE POTATOES-(SWITZERLAND)

(Pictured, page 55)

6 medium potatoes (about 2 pounds)
   steamed or boiled
2 tablespoons melted butter
1 cup dry white wine
1-½ cups grated Swiss cheese
2 tablespoons flour
1/4 cup milk or light cream
1 teaspoon salt
dash each garlic salt and pepper
1/8 teaspoon nutmeg
Kirsch (optional)
1 teaspoon dried chives

Cook cooked potatoes into chunks. Transfer to hot serving dish. Drizzle butter over potatoes. Keep warm in low oven. Heat wine in saucepan just until bubbles form on bottom of pan. With wooden spoon, stir in cheese, dredged with flour. Over medium heat, bring to boil, stirring constantly. Add milk. Season with salt, garlic salt, pepper, nutmeg and a splash of Kirsch, if desired. Pour over potatoes. Garnish with dried chives. 6 to 8 servings.

CRUSTY REDS AU POIVRE-(FRANCE)

(Pictured, page 55)

2 teaspoons sugar
2 pounds small red potatoes (about 12).
   steamed or boiled
1/4 cup butter or margarine
1 teaspoon salt
Pepper (preferably coarse grind)
3/4 cup bread crumbs*
Watercress or parsley for garnish

Sprinkle sugar in hot, heavy skillet. When melted, add cooked potatoes. Move pan continually over medium high heat to lightly brown potatoes on all sides. Add half of the butter and continue to move pan back and forth. Sprinkle salt, pepper and crumbs over potatoes, shaking pan to distribute and brown crumbs evenly. Turn into serving dish. Melt remaining butter in pan. Pour over potatoes. Garnish with watercress or parsley. Makes 6 to 8 servings.
*Whirl 1 slice white bread in blender.

ANCHOVY POTATO CASSEROLE (SCANDANAVIAN COUNTRIES)

(Pictured, page 55)

6 medium potatoes (about 2 pounds)
   steamed or boiled
1 can (2 ounces) rolled fillets of anchovies
4 green onions, chopped finely
3 tablespoons butter or margarine
1 tablespoon cornstarch
1-½ cups light cream or milk
1 teaspoon salt
dash pepper
pimiento and parsley for garnish

Cut cooked potatoes into large cubes and arrange in 2-quart casserole. Keep warm in low oven. Drain and chop 2 of the anchovies, reserving remaining for garnish. In small skillet, saute' chopped anchovies and green onions in butter. Mix together cornstarch and cream; then stir into butter. Bring slowly to boil, stirring. Add salt and pepper; simmer 2 minutes. Pour over potatoes. Garnish with pimiento, parsley and remaining anchovies. Makes 6 to 8 servings.

CURRIED POTATOES 'N' APPLES (GERMANY)

(Pictured, page 55)

1 can (1 pound) sauerkraut
6 medium potatoes (about 2 pounds)
   steamed or boiled
4 slices bacon
1/4 cup butter or margarine
2 red apples, unpeeled, sliced in rings
1/4 cup sliced almonds
½ teaspoon curry powder

Arrange sauerkraut in shallow 2-quart casserole. Quarter cooked potatoes lengthwise and arrange on top of sauerkraut. Keep warm in low oven. Fry bacon crisp; drain on paper towel; crumble. Add 2 tablespoons of the butter to drippings. Saute' apple rings a few at a time, until just tender. Arrange over sauerkraut with potatoes. Add remaining butter and curry to skillet. Heat until bubbly, stirring. Pour over all. Top with crumbled bacon and sliced almonds. Makes 8 servings.
Note: Casserole can be kept warm in low oven until serving time.

LIMA BEAN CASSEROLE

6 servings (2/3 cup each)
½ cup milk
1 cup celery, diced
1/4 cup parsley, finely chopped
3-½ ounce can french fried onion rings
10-½ ounce can condensed cheese soup
10-ounce package fordhook or baby lima beans,
    frozen, cooked

Preheat oven to 350 degrees F. (moderate). Grease a 1-½ quart casserole. Blend milk and soup. Add celery, parsley, and lima beans. Place mixture in casserole. Top with onion rings. Bake 45 minutes.

QUICK CANDIED SWEET POTATOES

6 servings
½ cup brown sugar, packed
½ teaspoon salt
2 tablespoons butter or margarine
½ cup syrup from sweetpotatoes.
dash cinnamon
23-ounce can drained sweetpotatoes

Combine all ingredients except sweetpotatoes. Cook over low heat for 5 minutes. Add sweetpotatoes and cook 15 to 20 minutes, turning occasionally.

PINEAPPLE-SWEET POTATO STACKS

2 cans (16 ounces each) sweet potatoes
1 can (15½ ounces) sliced pineapple
2 tablespoons brown sugar
2 tablespoons melted butter or margarine

Drain and mash sweet potatoes. Drain pineapple and save liquid. Combine sweet potatoes, 1/4 cup pineapple liquid, brown sugar and butter or margarine. Mix well. Arrange 6 to 8 pineapple slices in baking dish. "Tube" or spoon about 1/3 cup sweet potato mixture on each pineapple slice. Bake in a preheated moderate oven (350 degrees F.) about 10 minutes or until hot. 6 to 8 servings.

ORIENTAL VEGETABLE CROQUETTES

1 cup grated raw potatoes
3/4 cup coarsely grated carrots
½ cup chopped onion
1 clove garlic, minced
3/4 cup flour
1-½ teaspoons salt
1/4 teaspoon pepper
2 eggs, beaten
1/4 cup water
½ cup salad oil

Mix all ingredients together, except oil. Heat salad oil in fry pan and drop potato mixture by tablespoons into hot oil. Fry on both sides until golden brown. Drain on paper towel before serving.

SUMMER SQUASH BAKE

6 servings, 2/3 cup each
1 quart summer squash, sliced
1 teaspoon salt
2 eggs, beaten
½ cup breadcrumbs
½ cup water
1 cup medium white sauce
½ cup process cheddar cheese, shredded

Preheat oven to 350 degrees F. (moderate). Grease a 1-½ quart casserole. Cook squash in boiling, salted water for 5 minutes. Drain and use vegetable liquid to make the white sauce. Mix squash with white sauce and eggs. Place mixture in casserole. Sprinkle cheese and crumbs over the top. Bake for 25 minutes.

ORANGE-HONEYED ACORN SQUASH

6 servings (½ squash each)
3 small acorn squash
1/4 cup honey
1 teaspoon salt
1/8 teaspoon nutmeg (if desired)
2 tablespoons orange juice frozen concentrate
2 tablespoons butter or margarine

Preheat oven to 400 degrees F. Cut squash in half. Remove seeds. Place squash halves in a shallow baking pan. Combine orange juice concentrate, honey and salt. Mix well. Put some of the orange-honey mixture into each squash cavity. Add 1 teaspoon fat to each squash half. Sprinkle with nutmeg, if desired. Cover pan tightly with aluminum foil to keep steam in and speed cooking. Bake 30 minutes. Remove foil and continue baking 30 minutes more, or until squash is tender.

POTATO SALAD-AFRICAN HOT

2-½ pounds potatoes
½ cup olive oil
2 tablespoons fresh lemon juice
½ teaspoon salt
pinch cayenne pepper
3/4 cup sliced black olives
1 can (4 ounces) green chili peppers,
    seeded and chopped
1 medium Spanish onion, cut into small wedges

Boil potatoes in their jackets until tender. Chill for several hours, peel and dice them. In small mixing bowl combine olive oil, lemon juice, salt and cayenne pepper, mixing well. Add remaining ingredients to the olive oil mixture and pour over potatoes. Toss gently. Chill until ready to serve. Serve with Pimiento Dressing.

PIMIENTO DRESSING

2 cans (4 ounces each) pimientos, seeded
2 tablespoons sugar
1/3 cup mayonnaise
1-½ teaspoons lemon juice

Combine all ingredients in blender. Whirl until pimientos are pureed and all ingredients are thoroughly combined. Makes approximately 1-1/4 cups dressing.

CHICKEN-AVOCADO-RICE SALAD

6 servings, ½ cup each
4 teaspoons lemon juice
1 cup chicken, cooked, diced
½ cup celery, finely chopped
½ teaspoon green onion, finely chopped
1 teaspoon salt
1-½ cups avocado, diced
1 cup (about 1/3 cup uncooked) cooked rice
2 tablespoons mayonnaise
2 tablespoons sour cream
Lettuce leaves

Pour lemon juice over avocado. Combine remaining ingredients except lettuce. Mix well. Add avocado mixture and toss lightly. Chill. Serve on crisp lettuce.

MAKE-AHEAD SALAD OF RAW VEGETABLES

3/4 cup wine vinegar
½ cup olive oil
1/4 cup water
1 tablespoon sugar
1 teaspoon salt
½ teaspoon oregano
1/4 teaspoon pepper
1 small head cauliflower
2 carrots
1 or 2 green peppers
2 stalks celery
1/4 pound fresh mushrooms
3 ounces black olives, pitted
3 ounces stuffed olives
1 small jar pimiento
1 sweet red pepper, if available

Combine all cut up vegetables, into large pan, add vinegar, olive oil, water and seasonings. Bring to boil. Boil 5 minutes. Remove, and let cool. Refrigerate at least 24 hours. Drain liquid before serving.

ZESTY TWO-BEAN SALAD

2 packages (9 ounces each) frozen Italian beans,
    cooked and drained
1 can (15-½ ounces) garbanzo beans, drained
1/4 cup pieces ripe olives
1/4 cup strips red pepper or pimiento
½ cup Wish-Bone Italian Dressing
Lettuce or romaine

Combine Italian and garbanzo beans, ripe olives, red pepper or pimiento and Italian dressing. Chill. To serve, stir lightly and turn into bowl lined with lettuce or romaine.

POTATO SALAD-AFRICAN COOL

3-½ pounds potatoes
2 apples sliced into wedges
1 medium Spanish onion, cut into wedges
1-½ cups cheddar cheese, cubed
½ cup olive oil
3 tablespoons fresh lemon juice
½ teaspoon salt
pepper to taste
1/4 dry mustard

Boil potatoes in their jackets until tender. Chill for several hours; peel and dice. Place potatoes in a large bowl and add apple wedges, onion and cheddar cheese cubes. In a small bowl, combine remaining ingredients and beat well. Pour over salad and toss gently. Chill until ready to serve. 6-8 servings.

FRENCH KRAUT

1 quart grated cabbage
2 small onions
1 green pepper, chopped
½ cup sugar
½ teaspoon celery seed
½ teaspoon salt
3/4 teaspoon mustard seed
1/4 teaspoon turmeric
1/3 cup vinegar

Mix all ingredients together, refrigerate. A good substitute for a green salad occasionally.

TUNA WALDORF SALAD

2 cans (6-½ or 7 ounces each) tuna
1 cup diced apples
½ cup chopped celery
1/4 cup chopped nutmeats
½ cup mayonnaise or salad dressing
Lettuce

Drain tuna. Break into large pieces. Combine all ingredients except lettuce. Serve on lettuce. Serves 6.

TURKEY BUFFET SALAD

3 cups julienne strips cooked turkey breast
2 medium tomatoes, peeled
1 medium avocado, peeled
3 hard-cooked eggs
½ pound crisp, cooked bacon
½ cup crumbled blue cheese or finely grated cheddar
2 tablespoons finely chopped chives
½ head lettuce
1 small bunch chicory or red lettuce
1 head romaine
½ bunch watercress
1 cup garlic French dressing

Cut turkey breast into julienne strips. Finely chop tomatoes, avocado, eggs and bacon. With a sharp knife, chop each of the greens very fine. Spread in layers in large salad bowl, heaping up slightly in center. Arrange the turkey, tomatoes, avocado, eggs, bacon, cheese and chives in rows in pretty, contrasting colors over the top of the greens. For an especially attractive pattern, arrange turkey strips across center and on either end, then arrange tomato, egg, bacon in rows on one side of the center, with grated cheese, avocado and chives on the other; sprinkle bacon on either side of the breast of turkey.

To keep the attractive design while serving, sprinkle part of the dressing across only one end at a time, toss lightly and serve from that section. Makes 3-1/4 quarts salad or 8 to 10 servings.

KIDNEY BEAN SALAD

6 servings, about 3/4 cup each
½ teaspoon salt
½ cup vinegar
4 cups dry kidney beans, cooked, drained
   (about 1-½ cups uncooked)
2 eggs, hard-cooked, sliced
3/4 cup sugar
3 tablespoons cooking oil
½ cup celery, diced
½ cup green pepper, thinly sliced
1/4 cup onion, thinly sliced

Combine salt, sugar, vinegar, and cooking oil; mix well. Add vegetables and mix gently. Chill for at least an hour. Pour off liquid. Gently stir in eggs before serving.

NORTHWEST FRUIT SLAW

1 (16 ounce) can light sweet cherries
1 (16 ounce) can dark sweet cherries
3 fresh Anjou, Bosc or Comice pears
2 cups finely shredded cabbage
Creamy Fruit Mayonnaise (recipe below)
Lettuce

Drain cherries and remove pits. Reserve a few cherries for garnish. Core and slice 1 pear. Core and slice remaining pears into wedges for garnish. Combine cabbage, cherries and diced pear. Add Creamy Fruit Mayonnaise and toss lightly to coat fruit and cabbage. Place in a lettuce-lined bowl. Garnish with pear wedges and reserved cherries. 6 to 8 servings.

CREAMY FRUIT MAYONNAISE

1/3 cup mayonnaise
1/3 cup dairy sour cream
1 tablespoon honey
2 teaspoons lemon juice
1 tablespoon orange juice

Combine above ingredients, blending well. Makes 3/4 cup.

HARVEST WALDORF SALAD

1 can (13-1/4 ounces) pineapple chunks
Tangy Waldorf Dressing*
2 Washington Red Delicious apples
2 Washington Golden Delicious apples
1 cup chopped celery
½ cup slivered almonds, toasted
lettuce leaves

Drain pineapple, reserving syrup. Prepare Tangy Waldorf Dressing and reserve. Core and dice apples. Combine apples, pineapple, celery and almonds. Mix with Tangy Waldorf Dressing and serve in a lettuce lined bowl. 8 servings.
Note: Garnish salad with apple wedges dipped in pineapple syrup, if desired.

*TANGY WALDORF DRESSING

2 eggs
1/4 cup reserved pineapple syrup
1/4 cup sugar
2 tablespoons lemon juice
½ cup dairy sour cream

Beat eggs until light; add reserved pineapple syrup, sugar and lemon juice. Cook in a double boiler, stirring constantly, until thick. Remove from heat and cool. Fold sour cream into cooked egg mixture. Yield 1 cup.

FRENCH DRESSING

1-10-½ ounce can tomato soup
½ cup sugar
3/4 cup vinegar
1 teaspoon salt
1 teaspoon dry mustard
1 cup oil
clove garlic
dash Worcestershire sauce

Mix dry ingredients first, add remaining ingredients, beat until well blended. Serve as French dressing, plain, or add crumbled roquefort cheese or Blue cheese. Let stand for a few days in refrigerator.

WATERCRESS/PARSLEY SALAD DRESSING

1 bunch watercress
1 small bunch parsley
1/3 cup commercial mayonnaise
1/3 cup commercial sour cream
2 tablespoons milk
1-½ teaspoons lime juice

Remove stems from watercress and parsley and coarsely chop leaves. Place watercress and parsley in blender along with remaining ingredients. Whirl until completely blended and pureed. Makes approximately 1-1/4 cups dressing.

SPECIAL SALAD DRESSING

1 cup oil
½ cup sugar
1 tablespoon mustard
1 teaspoon salt
1/8 teaspoon pepper
½ teaspoon paprika
1 can tomato soup
½ cup vinegar
1 tablespoon Worcestershire sauce

Mix in blender until smooth and velvety. Makes 1-½ cups.

DESSERTS
SPECIALLY SELECTED TO SATISFY YOUR SWEET TOOTH.
A PERFECT CONCLUSION TO A GOOD MEAL.

PEAR RASPBERRY CHIFFON PIE

1 can (29 ounces) Bartlett pear halves
1 package (10 ounces) frozen raspberries
4 teaspoons unflavored gelatin
2 tablespoons lemon juice
½ cup heavy cream, whipped

Dash salt
3 egg whites
1/4 cup sugar
Baked 9-inch pastry shell

Drain pears, reserving 1/4 cup syrup. Puree enough pears to make 1 cup. Slice and set aside remaining pear halves for garnish. Defrost and drain raspberries, reserving a few whole berries. Add water to raspberry syrup to make 2/3 cup. Soften gelatine in reserved 1/4 cup pear syrup. Heat pureed pears and add softened gelatine to dissolve. Cool. Stir in lemon juice and raspberry syrup. Chill until partially set. Whip gelatine until thick and frothy. Fold in raspberries and whipped cream. Add salt to egg whites; beat until soft peaks form. Gradually add sugar and beat to stiff peaks. Fold into raspberry mixture. Pile into cooled pastry shell. Chill until firm. Before serving, garnish with reserved pear slices and raspberries. Makes 6 to 8 servings.

FROZEN MINT JULEP PIE

1-1/3 cups crushed chocolate wafers
2 tablespoons sugar
1/4 cup melted butter
1 envelope unflavored gelatin
½ cup sugar
1/8 teaspoon salt
3 eggs, separated
1 cup light cream or half and half
1/3 cup bourbon
3 tablespoons mint-flavored jelly
1 cup heavy cream, whipped
Few drops green food coloring

Combine crumbs, 2 tablespoons sugar and melted butter. Shape a square of aluminum foil into a 9-inch pie plate and press crumb mixture firmly into bottom and against sides of foil-lined pan. Chill. Combine gelatin, 1/4 cup sugar and salt in saucepan. Beat egg yolks lightly, add to light cream and bourbon and stir into gelatin mixture. Cook over low heat, stirring constantly, until custard coats the spoon. Stir in jelly. Chill until mixture begins to thicken. Beat egg whites to soft peaks. Gradually beat in 1/4 cup sugar; beat until meringue stands in peaks. Fold meringue and whipped cream into the thickened custard. Turn into crumb crust. Place in freezer until solid. Remove pie in foil panliner from pie plate, cover top and then overwrap with Heavy Duty Reynolds Wrap. Return pie to freezer. To serve, remove overwrapping, place pie in foil liner in pie plate, rolling foil to edge of plate. Garnish with whipped cream and sprigs of fresh mint, if desired. Serves 8 to 10.

LEMON MERINGUE PIE

9-inch pie, 6 to 8 servings
1 cup sugar
1/4 teaspoon salt
3 egg yolks, beaten
2 teaspoons lemon rind, grated
1 recipe meringue
1/3 cup cornstarch
2 cups water
2 tablespoons butter or margarine
1/3 cup lemon juice
1 baked pastry shell (9-inch)

Prepare pastry. Mix sugar, cornstarch, and salt in a saucepan. Gradually stir in water. Cook over medium heat, stirring constantly, until thickened. Cook 1 minute longer. Stir a little of the hot mixture into the egg yolks; then stir yolks into remaining hot mixture. Cook 1 minute longer, stirring constantly. Overcooking may thin the mixture. Remove from heat. Blend in fat, lemon rind, and juice. Pour warm filling into pie shell, top with meringue, and bake immediately.

DEEP DISH CHERRY PIE

6 to 8 servings
2 cans (16 ounces each) cherries, pitted red sour
1/8 teaspoon almond extract
1-3/4 cups sugar
3 tablespoons cornstrach
1 baked pastry shell, 9-inch

Preheat oven to 400 degrees F. (hot). Prepare pastry. Roll out in a square shape to cover a 9x9x2 inch pan. Make small slits to let steam escape during baking. Mix ingredients together lightly. Put mixture into pan. Top with crust. Bake 60 minutes or until crust is browned.

APPLE CRUNCH

4 cups sliced apples
4 tablespoons brown sugar
3 tablespoons flour
½ teaspoon cinnamon

In greased baking dish, place fruit. Combine sugar, flour and cinnamon. Sprinkle over fruit, stirring in a bit with a fork.

TOPPING

1 egg, well beaten
1 cup sifted flour
1 cup granulated sugar
1 teaspoon baking powder
1/4 teaspoon salt
½ cup melted butter

Beat egg until thick and lemon-colored. Combine all ingredients except butter, into flour, sifted, into beaten egg. Use table fork and mix until very crumbly. Sprinkle crumbly mixture over top of apples but do not mix in. Drizzle the melted butter over the top of the crumbly mixture. Bake in 375 degree F. oven for 45 minutes. Makes 6-8 servings. Serve warm. Very good with vanilla ice cream.

GOLDEN TRIFLE

1-4-½-ounce package vanilla pudding and
   pie filling
3-½ cups milk
4 teaspoons sherry
1/8 teaspoon almond extract
1-7-½ ounces package jelly rolls cut in
   12 slices
Orange slices, cut in half, drained
Maraschino cherries, chopped, drained

Prepare mix as directed for pudding except use 3-½ cups milk. Cool. Stir in sherry and almond extract. Arrange dessert roll slices on bottom and sides of 1-½-quart glass bowl. Pour pudding over slices; chill. Arrange fruit on top before serving. 8 servings.

INDIVIDUAL BAKED CUSTARD

4 cups milk
6 eggs, slightly beaten
½ cup sugar
½ teaspoon salt
2 teaspoons vanilla
1/4 cup coconut, toasted

Scald milk; cool 3 to 5 minutes. Combine milk, eggs, sugar, salt and vanilla. Pour milk mixture into eight to ten 6-ounce custard cups; set in large shallow pan on oven rack. Pour hot water into pan to 1-inch depth. Bake in a preheated 325 degree F. oven 40 to 45 minutes or until knife inserted near center comes out clean. Cool. Refrigerate. Top with coconut before serving. 8 to 10 servings.
VARIATION: Pour milk mixture into 1-½-quart shallow baking dish instead of 6-ounce custard cups. Bake about 60 minutes.

POT DE CREME MOUSSE

1 package (6 ounce) semi-sweet chocolate pieces
1/4 cup sugar
1/4 cup water
1 tablespoon instant coffee
2 egg yolks, slightly beaten
1 teaspoon vanilla
2 egg whites
2 tablespoons sugar
½ cup whipping cream
chocolate whipped cream

Heat chocolate, sugar, water and coffee in a heavy saucepan over low heat, stirring constantly, until chocolate is melted. Remove from heat; gradually beat into egg yolks. Stir in vanilla. Cool slightly. Beat egg whites until soft peaks form. Gradually add 2 tablespoons sugar and continue beating until stiff but not dry. Fold into chocolate mixture. Whip cream until stiff; fold into chocolate mixture. Pour into six 4-ounce serving dishes. Chill. Top with Chocolate Whipped Cream.

CHOCOLATE WHIPPED CREAM

Add 2 tablespoons cocoa and 2 tablespoons confectioners' sugar to 1 cup whipping cream. Chill 30 minutes. Whip until stiff. Add ½ teaspoon each, almond extract and vanilla. Yield: 2 cups

LIME CREAM FLUFF

Mold, 1-3/4 cup, 4 servings
1 package (3 ounce) lime flavor gelatin
2/3 cup boiling water
½ pint vanilla ice cream
Chocolate mint cordial

In a small mixing bowl pour boiling water over gelatin; stir until dissolved. Beat in vanilla ice cream until well blended. Turn into mold. Chill until firm. Top with chocolate cordial or syrup, if desired. 142 calories per serving of pudding. 45 calories for 1 tablespoon chocolate cordial or syrup.

GINGER PEAR PIE

6 fresh Western winter pears
1-½ cups gingersnap crumbs
½ cup brown sugar
½ cup melted butter
2 tablespoons flour

1 teaspoon cinnamon
1/8 teaspoon salt
Pecan halves
Pastry for one-crust 9-inch pie

Core and slice pears, leaving skins on; reserve several slices for garnish if desired. Layer half of pear slices on bottom of pastry. Combine remaining ingredients, except pecans. Spread half of the mixture over pears. Layer remaining pears and top with crumb mixture. Bake at 375 degrees for 50 minutes. During last 20 minutes of baking, arrange reserve pear slices and pecans on pie and continue baking. Makes 1 (9-inch) pie.

CHOCOLATE CAKE

Two 8-inch layers or one 9x12 cake, 12 servings
2 cups cake flour, unsifted or
   1-3/4 all-purpose flour, unsifted
1 teaspoon soda
3 ounces chocolate, unsweetened, melted
1 teaspoon vanilla
1-½ cups sugar
1 teaspoon salt
½ cup softened butter, margarine
   or shortening
2 eggs
1 cup sour milk or buttermilk

Preheat oven to 350 degrees F. (moderate). Grease and flour two 8-inch layer pans or one 9x12x2 inch cakepan. Mix dry ingredients thoroughly. Blend in fat, chocolate, eggs, vanilla, and one-half of the milk; beat 2 minutes at medium speed with a mixer or 300 strokes by hand. Add remaining milk; beat 2 minutes longer in mixer or 300 additional strokes by hand. Pour into pans. Bake 25 to 35 minutes until cake surface springs back when touched lightly. Cool on a rack a few minutes before removing from pan. When cool, frost if desired.

POUND CAKE

24 servings
3/4 cup butter or margarine
3 eggs
1/4 teaspoon almond or lemon extract
½ teaspoon baking powder
3/4 cup milk
1-½ cups sugar
1 teaspoon vanilla
2-2/3 cups cake flour, unsifted or
   2-1/3 cups all-purpose flour, unsifted
½ teaspoon salt

Preheat oven to 350 degrees F. (moderate). Grease and flour a 10-inch tube pan. Beat fat and sugar until light and fluffy. Add eggs and flavorings. Beat well. Blend dry ingredients and add alternately with the milk. Pour batter into pan. Bake 1 hour or until top springs back when lightly touched. Cool in pan on rack for 15 minutes. Remove from pan

BROILER FROSTING

For 9x12 inch cake, 12 servings
1/4 cup softened butter or margarine
1/4 cup light cream
½ cup brown sugar, packed
1 cup flaked coconut

Preheat broiler. Mix ingredients well. Spread on top of baked cake. Broil until bubbly, about 3 minutes.
Note: Chopped nuts may be used in place of coconut. Or use a combination of nuts and coconut.

ORANGE CREAM PIE

1 baked pie shell, 5-inch
Filling:
   1/4 cup sugar
   5 teaspoons cornstarch
   dash of salt
   2/3 cup milk
   1 egg yolk, slightly beaten
   1 tablespoon butter
   ½ teaspoon grated orange peel
   4 teaspoons orange juice
Meringue:
   1 egg white
   1/4 teaspoon vanilla extract
   dash of cream of tartar
   2 tablespoons sugar

To prepare filling: In a 1-quart saucepan combine sugar, cornstarch and salt; gradually add milk. Cook over medium heat; stirring constantly, until thickened. Cook 2 additional minutes. Blend a small amount of hot mixture into egg yolk; return all to pan. Cook 1 minute. (Do not boil.) Remove from heat; add butter, orange peel and juice. Pour into pie shell. Cover top with Meringue. To prepare Meringue: Beat egg white until frothy. Add vanilla and cream of tartar and beat until soft peaks form. Add sugar, 1 tablespoon at a time, and continue beating until stiff peaks form. Mound onto pie filling, making certain that meringue covers filling completely and is sealed to crust. Bake in preheated 350 degree F. oven 8 to 10 minutes or until meringue is golden. Cool on wire rack. Chill before serving. Makes 2 servings.
Note: Four 3-inch prepared tart shells can be substituted for 5-inch pie shell.

We gratefully acknowledge and appreciate the excellent suggestions and material supplied us by: National Live Stock and Meat Board, Chicago, Illinois; United Dairy Industry Association/American Dairy Association, Rosemont, Illinois; Pacific Kitchen, Seattle, Washington; The Potato Board, Denver, Colorado; and Turkey Information Service, Salt Lake City, Utah. Thanks also to Nancy Haus, Erie, Pa.

CHOCOLATE CAKE

Two 9-inch layers or one 9x12 cake, 12 servings
2 cups cake flour, unsifted or
1-3/4 all-purpose flour, unsifted
1 teaspoon soda
3 ounces chocolate, unsweetened, melted
1 teaspoon vanilla
1-1/2 cups sugar
1 teaspoon salt
1/2 cup softened butter, margarine
or shortening
2 eggs
1 cup sour milk or buttermilk

Preheat oven to 350 degrees F. (moderate). Grease and flour two 8-inch layer pans or one 9x12x2 inch cake pan. Mix dry ingredients thoroughly. Blend in fat, chocolate, eggs, vanilla, and one-half of the milk; beat 2 minutes at medium speed with a mixer or 300 strokes by hand. Add remaining milk; beat 2 minutes longer in mixer or 300 additional strokes by hand. Pour into pans. Bake 25 to 35 minutes until cake surface springs back when touched lightly. Cool on a rack a few minutes before removing from pan. Then cool. Frost if desired.

POUND CAKE

24 servings
3/4 cup butter or margarine
3 eggs
1/4 teaspoon almond or lemon extract
1/2 teaspoon baking powder
3/4 cup milk
1-1/2 cups sugar
1 teaspoon vanilla
2-2/3 cups cake flour, unsifted or
2-1/3 cups all-purpose flour, unsifted
1/4 teaspoon salt

Preheat oven to 350 degrees F. (moderate). Grease and flour a 10-inch tube pan. Beat fat and sugar until light and fluffy. Add eggs and flavorings. Beat well. Blend dry ingredients and add alternately with the milk. Pour batter into pan. Bake 1 hour or until top springs back when lightly touched. Cool in pan on rack for 15 minutes. Remove from pan.

BROILER FROSTING

For 9x12 inch cake, 12 servings
1/4 cup soft butter or margarine
1/4 cup light cream
1/2 cup brown sugar, packed
1 cup flaked coconut

Preheat broiler. Mix ingredients well. Spread on cake. Broil until bubbly, about 3 minutes. Note: Chopped nuts may be used in place of a combination of nuts and coconut.

ORANGE CREAM PIE

1 baked pie shell, 8-inch
Filling:
1/4 cup sugar
3 teaspoons cornstarch
dash of salt
2/3 cup milk
1 egg yolk, slightly beaten
1 tablespoon butter
1/2 teaspoon grated orange peel
4 teaspoons orange juice
Meringue:
1 egg white
1/4 teaspoon vanilla extract
dash of cream of tartar
2 tablespoons sugar

To prepare filling: In a 1-quart saucepan, cornstarch and salt; gradually add milk. Cook, heat stirring constantly, until thickened, 2 minutes. Blend a small amount of hot mix, return all to pan. Cook 1 minute. (Do not cook) from heat; add butter, orange peel and juice shell. Cover top with Meringue. To prepare egg white until frothy. Add vanilla and cream beat until soft peaks form. Add sugar, 1 tablespoon, and continue beating until stiff peaks form onto pie filling, making certain that meringue completely and is sealed to crust. Bake in moderate degrees F. oven 8 to 10 minutes or until meringue is delicately browned.
Cool on wire rack. Chill before serving.
Note: Use an 8-inch prepared pie shell for a 3-inch pie shell.

We gratefully acknowledge and appreciate the excellent suggestions and recipes supplied to us by the Meat Board, Chicago, Illinois; United Dairy Industries Association; Poultry and Egg National Board; National Kitchen, Seattle, Washington; The Potato Board, Denver, Colorado; and the American Federation Services. Thanks also to Nancy Haus, Erie, Pa.